"WELCOME TO RAVEN CASTLE"

The big black bird squawked and launched itself at Stephen. He drew back, feeling the wind from its wings. The bird caught up short just before its claws could strike Stephen in the chest.

"Back, Fafnir!" Fell reeled the bird back with a chain attached to its leg.

"A most interesting pet, eh? A raven—found here at the Castle. The place lives up to its name. I've found many ravens here, and I've amused myself by training them."

"Kill him! Kill him!" the raven croaked.

ESCAPE FROM RAVEN CASTLE

J.J. Fortune

RACE AGAINST TIME™

Special thanks to
Olga Litowinsky, George Nicholson, Bruce Hall,
Betsy Gould, Beverly Horowitz, and Helene Steinhauer
from J.J. Fortune and others.

Published by
Dell Publishing Co., Inc.
1 Dag Hammarskjold Plaza
New York, New York 10017

Cover illustration by Bob Larkin
Interior illustrations by Bill Sienkiewicz
Map by Giorgetta Bell McRee

Laurel-Leaf Library ® TM 766734, Dell Publishing Co., Inc.

ISBN: 0-440-92406-5

RL: 6.2

Printed in the United States of America

First printing—January 1984

To my father,
my first—and favorite—storyteller

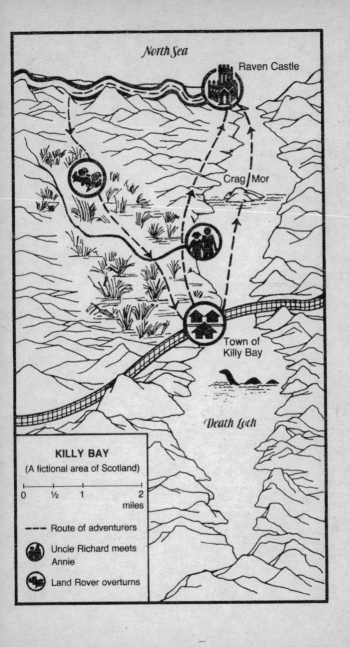

North Sea

Raven Castle

Crag Mor

Town of
Killy Bay

Death Loch

KILLY BAY

(A fictional area of Scotland)

0   ½   1   2
                miles

- - - Route of adventurers

Uncle Richard meets
Annie

Land Rover overturns

CONTENTS

1

STRANGERS ON A TRAIN

SATURDAY: 5:03 P.M., *Scotland*

Stephen Lane woke up with a start. Had he heard something? He blinked in the dark train compartment. How long had he sat dozing in his seat? It seemed like just moments ago he'd drowsily watched the sunlight on the Scottish mountains. What time was it?

He tried to look at his high-tech wristwatch. It could do just about anything if you pressed the right buttons. Stephen hoped he remembered the combination that lit up the dial. He was wrong. A thin beam of light shot out from the dial instead. It framed the scene across the compartment like a spotlight.

A man had his hands around Uncle Richard's throat. The strangler's beefy face reddened as he tightened his grip. Stephen sat up in horror.

The train thundered into daylight. They'd been in a tunnel. Now Stephen saw a second man, who was standing in the doorway. "Get 'im, Dougal," he shouted, shaking his fist. With his pinched features and red hair he looked like a fox. "Choke the life out of 'im!"

"Yeah, Davey." Dougal pushed hard, pressing Uncle Richard back into his seat. The big man grinned in triumph.

Then Uncle Richard's hands flew up to clap painfully over Dougal's ears.

"Ooooch!" said Dougal, bringing his own hands to his head. Uncle Richard drew a gasping breath and sank his fist in the big man's belly. Dougal folded over, and Uncle Richard brought his elbow down on the back of the man's head. As Dougal sank to the floor Uncle Richard jumped to his feet.

Davey, the fox-faced little man, was paralyzed with surprise for a second. Then he reached into the pocket of his cheap leather jacket and whipped out a knife. "Ye'll stay where you are, or I'll have yer hide," he snarled, stalking into the compartment.

Still gasping for air, Uncle Richard wobbled on his feet. But his eyes had a hard, angry look, like two smooth gray pebbles. Stephen knew that look meant trouble. "Get out," Uncle Richard said, his voice harsh from the rough treatment to his throat, "or I'll take care of you the way I took care of this clown."

Davey lunged with his knife, feinting at Uncle Richard's eyes, then coming in for a stab at the chest. Uncle Richard dodged and threw a punch. But Davey wasn't there. "So," he said, "it comes down to who hits the other one first." He grinned and suddenly shifted his knife to his other hand.

All through this Stephen sat frozen in shock. Now he roused himself as he saw Dougal shakily getting up on his hands and knees. The groggy goon had his back to Stephen, presenting an excellent target. Stephen remembered a scene from an old John Wayne movie. He wound up and kicked Dougal in the seat of his pants. It felt like kicking a wall, and it didn't work the way it had for John Wayne. Dougal just roared and swept his arm behind him. His fist hit Stephen like a wrecker's ball and smashed him into the outside door of the train compartment.

Stephen's elbow banged into the handle, the door opened, and he tumbled out of the carriage.

"Yaaaaah!" Stephen cried, expecting to hit the ground at high speed. He squeezed his eyelids tight, trying to shut out the end. Instead, he was surprised to find himself rolling along a flat surface. His eyes popped open to see a station platform, and the train puffing to a stop. Stephen jumped to his feet and ran off shouting. "Help! Help! Somebody! Two men are trying to kill my uncle!"

A pair of big men with black beards came striding down the platform. Stephen had a moment of hope, but they brushed right past him. Through the open compartment door he saw them plunge in and tackle his uncle. In desperation Stephen turned to the small,

15

shabbily dressed crowd around the station. "Somebody! Help him! Please!"

The people stood still for a moment. A man in a checked cloth cap made a fist and took a step forward. Then everyone abruptly looked away.

"What's the matter with you?" Stephen yelled.

Right at that moment a man came flying out of the carriage door. It was Foxy-face, the one called Davey. He landed on the platform with a thud and shook his head, trying to clear it. Then he saw Stephen and shot out his hand. Clawlike fingers clamped around Stephen's ankle. "I got the little perisher!" Davey cried. "I'll hold him out here!" He stood up and transferred his hold to Stephen's arm. "Better than going back to fight that flamin' madman," he muttered.

Dougal came reeling back out of the train, followed by one of the black-bearded men. The other one stood in the doorway, trying to defend himself as Uncle Richard pounded maniacally at him. Stephen was amazed at the look of fury on his uncle's face as he tried to fight his way through the door.

The train lurched forward. Uncle Richard lost his footing and Blackbeard threw a last desperate punch, knocking Uncle Richard backward into the compartment. The train began to pick up speed.

Stephen wrenched free of Davey's grasp and ran after the train. His eyes were fixed on the open door as he pounded along the station platform. He never saw Dougal come up behind him. A huge hand yanked him up by the shirt collar.

"Uncle Richaaaard!" Stephen screamed. But the train was moving too fast for Uncle Richard to do anything. It shrieked around a short curve and chugged onto a hulking stone-and-steel bridge over a leaden expanse of water.

Stephen hung from Dougal's hand, paralyzed. He can't get off the train! He can't come back to save me!

From behind him he heard Davey's voice. "Put 'im in the car, Dougal," With that Stephen came alive again. He squirmed, making a grab at the signpost that hung from the station roof. For a moment he held on, his face pressed to the town name, KILLY BAY. But Dougal easily tore him away. Stephen kicked out at Dougal, screaming to the townspeople, "Please! Help me! PLEASE!"

But Dougal held him out at arm's length and Stephen's feet couldn't reach any vital parts. As for the people in the marketplace, they didn't move.

Dougal hustled over to a big black car, pulled open the back door, and tossed Stephen in as if he were a puppy. Then he got in and sat down as Davey came in the other side. The two blackbeards sat in the front seat, one holding a bloody handkerchief to his nose. "Ah fink he brook it, Davey," he said as the car started up.

"Probably fell on it and broke it yourself, you clumsy clod," Davey said.

"Where are you taking me?" Stephen burst out.

Davey thrust his face into Stephen's. All he could

17

see was the man's bloodshot eyes. "Put a sock in it, kid. Ye'll find out soon enough."

The car roared off in the opposite direction from the bridge, through a marketplace, and soon left the town behind. Jerking this way and that, it made its way along a winding road to the top of a cliff. Far below, grayish water swirled.

"Death Loch looks calm today," said Bloody Nose.

"You shutcher noise too!" Davey snapped. Bloody Nose shut up. But the mention of the Death Loch stirred Stephen's memory.

It was something Uncle Richard had mentioned on the train. *Just before we get to Carrabash, we'll go across a sea loch—Loch Killy. About forty years ago all the fish in the loch died. Nothing, not even weeds, has grown there since. They call the place the Death Loch.*

So now I know where I am, Stephen thought. The only problem is, what are they going to do with me?

Stephen rocked between his silent captors as the car zigzagged along the cliff road. The lake below looked even gloomier. He huddled into himself and tried to get some sort of clue to the mystery.

What do they want with me? he asked himself. Obviously it must have something to do with Uncle Richard. Stephen shivered. *I hope they don't want to get any of his secrets out of me.*

2

BORED, BORED, BORED ...

FRIDAY: 8:17 P.M., *New York*

The fact was, Stephen hardly knew anything about Uncle Richard. He'd just turned up on the steps of the family brownstone in New York one day. The folks were happy to have him—but this apparently mild-mannered uncle, it turned out, had a lot more to him than they knew.

Uncle Richard had said he was an engineer. But Stephen learned that he blew up a lot more bridges than he built. The first time Stephen's parents left him with Uncle Richard for a weekend, Uncle Richard's wild past had reached out to get them involved in a risky two-day adventure, *Revenge in the Silent Tomb*. This time it had gotten Stephen stranded in Scotland.

Stephen let out a long breath. At last he was

thinking again. Okay, it had something to do with Uncle Richard. What had he said about this trip? Stephen wrinkled his brow, remembering. It was after dinner on Friday, last night.

Uncle Richard had stood by the door, saying good-bye to Stephen's mother and father. "These people at Fell Industries really know how to do things first class," Dad said. "They're giving me a free trip to San Francisco to talk to them, and they even invited Marion along." He smiled at his wife. "Even if I did have to twist her arm to get her out of that health-food store of hers."

"I wish you'd stop making jokes about Oh, Nuts!" Mom flared at Dad. Then she turned back to Uncle Richard. "You're sure everything will be fine?"

"Positive, Marion," Uncle Richard said.

"You won't let Stephen get into any trouble."

"Of course not. *Ha, ha, ha.*"

To Stephen's eyes Uncle Richard's smile was definitely fishy. I've seen this guy handle bombs like they were nothing, he thought. But he gets all nervous when he talks with my mother.

Dad picked up the bags, and he and Mom went out to the taxi. Stephen and Uncle Richard waved good–bye. They saw Mom's blond head looking back at them until the cab disappeared into the traffic.

Uncle Richard walked back into the living room

and did something odd—he threw himself onto the sofa and lay down, sighing. "Are you okay, Uncle Richard?" Stephen asked.

Uncle Richard stretched his arms. "I've been here a couple of months, and every day is beginning to seem the same. I get up, putter in my workshop, go to the athletic club or the pistol range. I buy some books or take in a gallery opening and look at the pretty pictures. Perhaps, if I'm lucky, there's an old crony in town and we have lunch, or even better, an old enemy, so I have to watch my step. I'm bored, bored, bored. . . ."

Stephen sat down in a chair facing him. "We have a weekend all to ourselves."

Uncle Richard covered his eyes with his arm. "Last time we had one of those, you nearly got stung by scorpions."

"I don't think you're happy unless a bunch of crooks is chasing you," Stephen said. "There are lots of things we could do this weekend."

"Name three."

"How about seeing a basketball game with Jerry? His Dad's company has box seats at Madison Square Garden."

"I like your friends—but basketball?" Uncle Richard was not impressed.

"We could go down to Chinatown. You promised you'd take me to the restaurant that serves yak stew."

"Mmm," Uncle Richard said.

"There's a great double feature playing a couple of blocks from here. *Raiders of the Frost* and *Finders of the Dark*."

"Nnnnn. I wish you'd stop trying to take me to silly films like those. After all, you were there watching while Jack Hartford shot *The Deep, Dark Secret.* You should know by now how unrealistic they are."

Stephen went into a shocked silence. No movie was ever silly—at least, not till he'd seen it the fourth or fifth time. He could never understand Uncle Richard's attitude. Unrealistic? That was the best thing about movies. They were *better* than reality.

He was opening his mouth for a hot reply when the phone rang. "Get that, Steve," Uncle Richard said. Then he snapped gracefully to his feet and reached for the phone. "Never mind."

He picked up the receiver and said hello. As he listened, a change came over his features. The half smile disappeared, and the lines around his eyes grew deeper. His whole face seemed to harden. Uncle Richard put the phone down and looked at it thoughtfully. "That was a telegram from an old friend of mine. He asks if I can meet him at the railway station at Carrabash by 5:15 tomorrow evening."

"Where's Carrabash?" Stephen asked.

"Near the northern tip of Scotland."

"Tomorrow evening? Are you going to go?"

"That's what I've got to find out." Uncle Richard looked at his watch, a twin to Stephen's, and began hitting tiny buttons around the outside of the case. Letters and numbers glowed on the dial—a name and phone number. "With good programming, you can get a lot into these watches," he said.

Stephen looked on in fascination. "When are you going to teach me all the secrets in that thing? You gave me one, but now I need an owner's manual."

"The Kronom K-D2 is not a toy," Uncle Richard said. "There are some dangerous gadgets in there."

"It's not likely I'll find out about them. Who'll tell me? Three of these watches in the world, and we own two of them. I wonder if we'll ever see the third one."

"If you do, I hope it won't be used against you," Uncle Richard said, picking up the receiver and dialing. "Hello, Lou. Richard Duffy here. Got an urgent request. What would you say if I told you I needed a seat on the next flight to Glasgow?" He winced as he listened. "I thought you might say something like that. But if I have to call in favors, I'll call in favors. Remember that time in Bangkok when I . . ." He looked at Stephen and coughed. "I suppose I really shouldn't go into that." He nodded. "But you do remember? I need . . ."

"You're not going to leave me behind?" Stephen whispered.

Uncle Richard shrugged. ". . . two seats on that flight." Stephen smiled. "Don't start up again! Right. We'll need a connecting flight to Inverness. Do you have the railway schedule? Check the Highland Coastal Line—to arrive at Carrabash by 5:15.'' He looked up at Stephen. ''You sure you want to come?''

''I've always wanted to see Scotland,'' Stephen said.

Uncle Richard was back on the phone. ''Those schedules work out perfectly, do they? Well, well. One more thing. What have you heard about Hamish Claymore? Nothing since he retired from Intelligence? Thanks, Lou.'' Uncle Richard hung up.

''Hamish Claymore? Is that your old friend?'' Stephen said.

''Yes. I owe him.''

''He was in British Intelligence? Like James Bond?''

Uncle Richard's eyes came back to Stephen. ''I want you to forget that. He's in trouble, and he wants us to meet him at a railway station. Knowing Hamish, he'll probably contact us on the train. We've got to make sure we're on it.'' He headed for the stairs. ''Bring your passport and one small bag—things you can afford to lose. Meet me in five minutes. We have to move it to make all these connections.''

For almost the next sixteen hours, they had traveled. Most of that time was spent in a boring night flight to Glasgow. In the early morning they landed and bounced through a wild drive to another airport for the local flight to Inverness. Uncle Richard hadn't said another word about Hamish Claymore. But after they

24

got on the train at Inverness, he sat facing the door of the compartment, looking up expectantly whenever anyone passed by.

So what does that tell me? Stephen wondered now, staring out the window of the car as it weaved past a rocky headland. My kidnapping must have something to do with Hamish Claymore, and I don't know a thing about him.

The narrow road curved suddenly, leading out onto the headland itself. Stephen looked down. The loch was no longer calm. The sea must be nearby. He didn't see a tree, a bush, or a blade of grass—just stark, brown stone beaten by the waves below.

The car roared around another curve and Stephen blinked in surprise. At the tip of the headland stood a castle, or what was left of one. The walls and towers were made of the same brown stone as the cliffs, but time had taken its toll. The old keep still rose about six stories tall, but two of the towers at its corners had fallen into ruin. Behind it stood more walls. Huge sections of brown stone had tumbled down, revealing glassless windows and roofless buildings—empty shells, open to the sky. It looked like a castle with leprosy, a diseased growth on the battered rock.

The car came straight up the path, past a ruined gatehouse, and onto a long, narrow stone bridge. Obviously it was built for horses rather than for cars. Stephen watched the stone walls of the bridge whiz close by. Then the car went barreling through a gateway and into a courtyard. Iron bars slammed like a guillotine into the ground behind them. That sort of stuff went out with knights in armor, Stephen thought. What am I getting into here?

3

THE DEATH MERCHANT

SATURDAY: 5:30 P.M., *Scotland*

The car screamed to a stop in the courtyard of the castle. Dougal and Davey yanked Stephen out. Each holding an arm, they marched him into the building. Stephen tried to slow down since he'd never seen the inside of a real castle before. He had a hard time taking all this seriously—it was like a crazy dream.

The duo dragged him first through a maze of dirty stone corridors, then into spotless, expensively decorated rooms. It was chilly inside in spite of the warm weather.

In one room he saw beautiful antique furniture, swords and shields on the walls, and then a rocket displayed on a table. Boy, this guy has a weird interior decorator, Stephen thought.

They came to a large hall decorated just as queerly.

Suits of ancient armor stood beside mortars and heavy machine guns. When they passed a table covered with pistols and rifles, Stephen tried to edge over. Dougal gave him a shove that sent him sprawling onto another table, this one displaying knives and hand grenades.

"You idjit!" Davey yelled as he and Dougal rushed to grab Stephen. Dougal banged into the table. A shield fell from the wall and hit Davey on the head. He rubbed his scalp and glared at Dougal. Then they frisked Stephen and went on, keeping him well away from the tables.

If they weren't so scary, they'd be like Laurel and Hardy, Stephen thought.

Holding tightly to Stephen's collar, Dougal stood while Davey opened a big, brass-bound door at one end of the hall. The two men hustled him up a winding staircase that seemed to go on forever. Finally they came to a man standing beside another heavy wooden door. The man stepped aside and Dougal knocked. A voice said, "Come."

They entered a little round room. "Welcome to Raven Castle," said a tall old man seated by the fireplace.

He looks like a colonel in an old British war movie, Stephen thought. The man sat erect. His thinning white hair was carefully cut, his gray moustache clipped. He wore a hairy tweed suit. But British officers were supposed to be a healthy pink. This man was white as marble. Little purple lines under his skin showed where his veins were. His teeth looked like marble, too, showing faint veins of brown when he smiled.

The smile disappeared when the man saw that Stephen was alone. "Where is he?" he barked.

Davey wiped his palms on his trouser legs as he answered. "We fought hard, and got the lad, but, well, that is to say . . ." The officer's colorless eyes bored into him. "Er, 'e got away."

A cane whipped up from the side of the chair to hit Davey in the neck. "Fool!" Davey rubbed his neck and said nothing.

The colorless eyes stayed on him. "Take a car. Go to Carrabash. Meet Duffy on the platform and deliver my terms to him." The man's voice was like the breeze off an iceberg. "Don't fail me, Davey. Or you'll end up feeding my friend."

Stephen suddenly realized that the room had another occupant, a big black bird that spread its wings a yard wide. It cocked an eye at Davey. "Kill him! Kill him!" it screeched.

Dougal and Davey hurried to the door. Davey's fox-face was the color of oatmeal. The arrogant voice stopped them. "You shouldn't have a hard time." Stephen felt those weird eyes shift to him. "I'm sure Duffy will be only too glad to do what I want to save his dear nephew, Stephen."

That cold gaze made Stephen's skin crawl as the two thugs tumbled out. He knows who I am! he thought. But who is he? Other than being the Big Boss?

The man seemed to read his mind. "I'm Fell—Jonathan Fell. I'm a businessman, boy. I sell weapons. Wherever there's a war, I make money. Some people don't like that—they call me the Death Merchant. They can call me what they like—as long as their governments keep buying."

Fell's eyes seemed to turn inward. "I've known your uncle for a number of years. . . ." The eyes flicked back to Stephen. "You can see I don't consider him a friend. He doesn't like me . . . even ruined some business for me. But now he'll make up for that. I've got a little job for him. And he'll do it—because of you."

"What kind of a job?" Stephen asked.

Fell's cane rapped him sharply on the shin. "Don't interrupt, boy. It isn't polite."

Stephen bit back the answer he wanted to give. Since when has it been polite to hit people with a cane?

Fell went on. "He'll do a little diving for me. I want something that's down in the water of the loch. My men are afraid of the Death Loch—miserable cowards. But your uncle is a top-drawer diver. Did you know that? Used to salvage ships. He even did a dive for your government—getting secrets from the Soviet submarine *Volga* when it sank in the Sea of Japan. If he can handle a sunken nuclear sub, the Death Loch should be child's play for him."

He sat back, showing his decayed marbled teeth in a wintry smile. "Your uncle would never do it unless I had a hold over him. And I'd never had that until I heard that he'd rediscovered his family. So I arranged that your mother and father went off to San Francisco to discuss business with Fell Industries, and right after that your uncle gets an urgent cable. I knew he would come, and that he'd bring you. . . ." The cane flashed out again and poked Stephen in the chest. "You're my insurance, you see. I have you, and he does the work."

Just then the big black bird squawked and launched itself at Stephen. He drew back, feeling the wind from its wings. The bird caught up short just before its claws could strike Stephen in the chest.

"Back, Fafnir!" Fell reeled the bird back with a chain attached to its leg.

"A most interesting pet, eh?" The bird perched on the back of Fell's chair and began preening. "A raven—found here at Raven Castle. The place lives up to its name. I've found many ravens here, and I've amused myself by training them."

"Kill him! Kill him!" the raven croaked.

"Intelligent birds." Fell looked indulgent as the raven hopped onto his arm. "Would you like me to leave it with you? You could teach it some new words."

Stephen watched the beak and claws.

"Perhaps not," Fell went on, showing his marbled teeth again. "All you have to do is take it easy.

You'll get good meals, a pleasant place to stay . . .''
The cane swept around to show off the tower room.

Stephen stood quietly, wishing Fell would finish
his guided tour and go.

"I'm sure you're a clever enough lad not to go
thinking of ways to escape—it's quite impossible,
you know. And it would make me angry." Fell
tapped his cane on the stone floor.

"Just enjoy your stay—and your new home. This
tower has seen a lot of history. It even has a tradition.
No one has ever escaped from it—alive. I trust I
make myself clear."

Stephen nodded.

"Then good-bye for now." Fell rose from the
chair, the raven still perched on his arm. He walked
to the door and pounded on it with his cane. The
door opened. Fell smiled at Stephen again, and walked
out. The door slammed shut. Locks shot into place
with a muffled *clank*.

Stephen went to the door and put his ear to it.
"Rather stupid child," he heard Fell say. "As soon
as Duffy is at work in the loch, we'll dispose of
him."

4

LOCKED IN THE TOWER

SATURDAY: 5:50 P.M., *Scotland*

For a long moment Stephen stood with his ear pressed to the door. Finally he stepped away, his knees still weak.

Anyway he looked at it, his future looked grim—and short. Fell would kill him if he stayed there. Could Uncle Richard do anything? No. He'd have to play along to keep Stephen safe, and then it would be too late. Unless . . . Maybe Uncle Richard had planned for this. Again, no. He had looked too surprised on the train. Stephen stood in the middle of the room and made up his mind. He had to get out of here. I'm the insurance. If Fell can't threaten me, Uncle Richard won't work for him.

Stephen prowled around the room, trying to find a way out. His first choice was the door. The lock was old and clumsy. Uncle Richard could probably pick it. Stephen could certainly try. But as he knelt to examine the lock, he heard someone moving beyond the door. Of course—the guard.

He turned to the window. Five iron bars were set into the windowsill. Stephen's heart sank. But there were still the walls and floor. Maybe he could find a weak spot or a secret passage.

Stephen ran his mind over all the prison movies he had seen, looking for ideas. He could carve a bar of soap to look like a gun . . . no, too unrealistic. Besides, he didn't have any soap. How had they gotten away in *Escape from Alcatraz*?

Then he went crazy, searching frantically for some kind of vent in the walls. Nothing. He lay on the floor for a moment, breathing heavily. When he looked at his watch, he was amazed at how much time had gone by. He had to admit two things. One, there's no way out of here. And two—Stephen brushed his hands on one of the curtains—nobody has cleaned this room in the last 400 years.

But trying to joke couldn't comfort him for long. No way out meant the end of Stephen Lane. He'd never see his home again. Home seemed unreal and far away right now, like something in a children's book.

Stephen roused himself to look around the brown stone walls of his prison, searching again for carvings or lines that would show a secret door. There weren't any. He tried pushing against the walls again. The stone blocks had a damp, faintly greasy feel. It made Stephen's skin crawl, but that was all. His shoulders sagged.

Stephen walked over to the window. Below him he could see crumbling walls, the cliff, and the seething gray waters of the Death Loch. Stephen's hands grasped the iron bars in the window. I've got to get out of here! He shook the bars in frustration.

One of them moved.

It didn't move a lot, but it did move. Stephen hurriedly went through his pockets. His captors hadn't taken anything away, probably thinking a "stupid child" couldn't give them trouble. He pulled out his key ring and chose the biggest one on it—his house key. For a second he stopped. A vision of his nice, safe front door at home appeared before his eyes. He shook his head. He'd never see it again if he didn't get to work.

Using the point of the key, he began scraping away at the bottom of the bar. The mortar of the windowsill crumbled surprisingly easily as he scraped. Stephen thought for a moment. He took the key and scraped between the blocks on the wall. He couldn't even scratch a line on that cement. Stephen dashed back to the windowsill and looked carefully at his work. It's like somebody already dug into this stuff, he said to himself.

Maybe no one had escaped from the tower, but at least one prisoner had tried. He'd gouged out the mortar at the base of the bars but hadn't been able to finish the job. Probably executed after loosening only one bar. That would be too small for a grown man. But for a skinny kid, it would be just right.

Two hours later Stephen had ruined his keys but cleared a groove that completely freed the loose bar. He grasped it at the bottom with both hands and braced a foot against the wall. "Here goes nothing," he muttered, and yanked. The bar grated against the stone, but it moved. Then Stephen tugged on the bar to free it at the top. The iron made a grumbling noise as it loosened in its socket. Stephen darted a glance at the door and tugged again.

The bar slipped out suddenly, nearly falling out the window onto the castle walls. With a heave Stephen twisted the bar so it fell softly onto the bed.

He ran back to the window and looked down at the castle walls. It was a long way down. He couldn't see any handholds, so he'd need a ladder or a rope. Stephen glanced around the room. No ladders or ropes in sight. He sat on the bed. His back ached from the hours he'd spent leaning over to scrape at that cement. He rubbed his spine, then rested his hand on the bedsheet.

Another old movie he'd seen popped into his head— *The Prisoner of Zenda*. Stephen remembered the hero tearing the bedclothes into strips to use as a rope ladder. Of course the hero had a sword to get the strips started. But Stephen had a more modern weapon.

He slipped his watch off his wrist and held it up. The Kronom K-D2 might look like an everyday watch, but it was a lot more—and here was a chance to use one of the gadgets hidden in it.

Stephen pressed a three-button combination on the side of the case. The watch crystal flipped up. Holding the watch carefully—that crystal was sharp!—Stephen started slicing.

It took a lot more time than it had in the movie. The heavy coarse linen didn't tear easily. Finally he had a pile of strips by the window. He tied them together, then fastened one end of the rope to a solid bar. Leaning through the opening, he threw the other end down. Would it reach? No time to worry—here I go. . . .

The climb down the tower was fairly easy, especially since the chinks between the stone blocks turned out to be perfect toeholds. The trip might have been fun, except that the rope seemed to have its own idea about how Stephen would reach the ground. The sheets that wouldn't rip upstairs now delighted in making tearing sounds. And Stephen wished he had taken a little more time with those knots.

Still, it wasn't too bad till he came to the first window under his. A black thunderbolt seemed to dart through the bars, aiming for his face. Raucous cries rang in Stephen's ears as he flung an arm up, trying to protect his eyes from the raven. "Kill him! Kill him!" the bird croaked. Dozens of other cries came from inside the room.

"Great. Fell's birdhouse," Stephen muttered.

With only one hand on the rope Stephen couldn't

move. But the raven couldn't get at his eyes. It looked like a standoff until the bird began pecking vigorously on the hand holding the rope.

"A very intelligent bird," he said, gritting his teeth. "I wonder if Fell taught you this trick."

Stephen hunched his head and loosened his grip on the rope. He dropped down past the window and grabbed tight again. He swore he could hear the rope tear somewhere above him, but it held. The raven squawked angrily. Chained to a perch, it could just barely get out the window. It couldn't hurt him now, unless the racket it was making caught somebody's attention. Stephen kept a wary eye on the window as he made his way down farther.

The raven turned its attack to the rope, its cruel beak slashing at the linen strip. Stephen could feel the sheet beginning to give.

His eyes glued to the raven, Stephen missed a foothold and spun sickeningly. His hands were white and he closed his eyes, trying not to think of the rocks far below.

He dug his toes into the wall frantically, stopping the spin. Then he heard the rope start to tear. He raced down recklessly, cursing the bird all the way. He was only ten feet from the top of the wall when the rope broke.

Stephen landed on his feet, flexing his knees to take the impact, and wound up on his rump. A perfect three-point landing, he thought as he stood, rubbing himself. Then he heard a voice. "Hey!

Wotcher doin' over there?'' A second's silence, then, "Blimey! It's the brat! 'E's gettin' away!''

That was all Stephen needed to hear. He bolted to his right along the ancient path on top of the wall where guards once walked their rounds. Ahead was an old door into the keep. Behind it he heard the tramp of rushing feet. He turned back the way he had come and ran at lung-bursting speed.

The bulge of the big tower blocked Stephen's view. He dashed around it and found himself on a stretch of straight castle wall. He legged it as fast as he could. Before him was a small guard tower. And beyond it the wall crumbled away. Stephen looked back. One man had come around the tower on the battlement, and he could hear more catching up.

Maybe if I get off the wall I could lose them there, he thought. He ran for the crumbled section of wall. But as he sprinted past the small guard tower door, a hand shot out of the shadows and grabbed his shoulder. He was caught.

5

THE BLACK STAIRCASE

SATURDAY: 8:16 P.M., *Scotland*

As he was yanked into the doorway, Stephen fought back, breaking the grasp of the mysterious hand. He leaped for the open doorway. The hand snatched after him, grabbing his arm.

"Do you really want to go back there?"

Stephen stared for a second. "Uncle Richard!" he gasped. "But how?"

"No time!" Uncle Richard hissed. The first pursuer had reached the small guard tower. "Get farther back," Uncle Richard whispered. Stephen slipped into the darkness.

The guard almost rushed past the doorway. Then he stopped, blinking into the darkness. "Just a kid," he muttered, stepping forward. His eyes nearly popped at the sight of the big, grown-up arm that snaked out of the darkness and yanked him in. A little too late, he went for the pistol holstered at his side. Uncle Richard's hand clamped over his right wrist, inches away from the gun butt. The guard opened his mouth to yell—and found a steely hand cutting off his air.

He tried to pull back, then braced one leg on the wall behind him and pushed with all his might.

Uncle Richard toppled, but brought the guard down with him. The fall broke Uncle Richard's hold, and Stephen could hear the guard gasp for breath. He threw a vicious punch at Uncle Richard, and connected. Uncle Richard fell back and the guard tore loose. With a *hah!* of victory he went for his gun again.

That was a mistake. As the guard rose up on his knees and unholstered the pistol, he was framed against the light of the doorway. Stephen leaped out of the darkness, swinging his leg up. He had aimed for the gun hand, but the guard heard him and turned so that Stephen's foot ended up in the pit of the guard's stomach. "*Guuuuuuurrrk!*" he said, flopping over.

Uncle Richard brought his fist up from the floor and hit the guard on the chin. His head snapped back, and the rest of his body followed it, right out the door of the tower. The gun clattered on the stone walkway.

At that moment the other pursuers arrived at the crumbled section of wall.

"There's Hal Perkins!" somebody yelled.

"Cor! What did that kid do to him?"

Stephen shrank into the darkness. "They'll see us if we step out of this tower."

"Stairway here. Let's go down," Uncle Richard said. "Move it."

But they found they couldn't move it very fast. The stairway in the tower wasn't built for hurrying. It was a spiral staircase made of the same stone as the tower. The stairway was also narrow—Uncle Richard's shoulders brushed against the sides as he went down—and the stairs themselves were tricky. They were steep and shaped like pieces of pie. Stephen had to watch where he walked.

To add to their troubles, the stairway hadn't been used in generations, and the steps were crumbling away like wedges of cheese nibbled by mice. Stephen could hardly see the steps in the gloom. An occasional slit window let a little half light in, but not enough to see anything properly.

Uncle Richard had taken the lead, saying, "If you fall, you'll just fall on me." Five steps down he'd almost gotten stuck in the narrow stairwell. "And we probably won't go far anyway," he added.

They continued picking their way down the stairs. Occasionally Uncle Richard hit a button on his watch to send out a thin beam of light ahead of them. Then they heard men's voices raised in argument above. "There's nowhere else he could have gotten to. He ain't on the wall. He had to go down these steps."

"Well, *I* ain't going down those steps. Like moldy

potatoes, they is. Could go to pieces right under yer feet.''

''I hope they believe him,'' Stephen whispered. A piece of stairway gave beneath his foot. ''I do.''

''We're goin' down to take a look,'' the first voice said. Stephen heard the tramp of heavy footsteps. Little pieces of broken stone came skittering down.

Stephen tried to hurry. He stayed close behind Uncle Richard, moving as quickly as possible. Then his heel landed on a chip of stone, and his leg flew out from under him. He cried out and slid down the stairs, hitting the backs of Uncle Richard's legs.

''What was that?'' said the first voice. The shower of debris came more heavily as the pursuers quickened their pace.

''Can't rush,'' Uncle Richard whispered, helping Stephen up. ''Not safe—''

''Watch out! The steps!'' someone yelled.

Stephen felt vibrations through the soles of his shoes. The heavy footfalls of the castle guards rattled through the whole staircase. He heard sounds of scrambling as good-sized chunks of stone came bouncing down. One of them hit him hard on the ankle. Then the whole section of steps around him crumbled to bits.

''The stairway is going,'' Stephen heard as he tumbled down the spiral. ''The brat is done for.''

6

A GETAWAY

SATURDAY: 8:28 P.M., *Scotland*

The fall made Stephen dizzy, as he was swept around in a spiral. Banging into the walls wasn't doing much for him either. And then there were those stones zinging down from above to hit him.

Stephen smacked into something. He bounced back and realized it was Uncle Richard, who had managed to brace himself in the narrow stairway. "Hold on!" Uncle Richard said. Stephen clasped his arms around his uncle's waist. Above him he could dimly see Uncle Richard's arms pushing straight against the walls.

Most of the debris that came rattling down the stairway ran harmlessly between their legs. But more came down relentlessly, pushing at them. Slowly they began to slide.

The pressure built up stronger than ever. Only Uncle Richard's hands and feet kept them from falling. He drew in a long, hissing breath, trying with all his might to hold them in place.

A big stone came bouncing down. Stephen heard the clatter as it struck behind him, and ducked. In the light from one of the slit windows he watched the chunk bounce on the wall in front of him and fly through the air again. It smashed into Uncle Richard's right wrist, then clattered on down.

"Agh!" Uncle Richard shouted. "Can't keep this hold . . ." His hand hung uselessly. They lurched forward with sickening speed. Uncle Richard tried to find a place to dig his heels into, but the stairs were too treacherous. Stephen flew under his uncle's legs and tumbled down in front of him.

Stephen's shoes slid along the smooth stone blocks. Then his right foot managed to dig into a crack. He lurched around, casting out his left foot until he found a hold on the opposite wall. The pressure of Uncle Richard's body and the rocks behind him was unrelenting. Stephen's leg muscles strained, bunched, and knotted. For a heart-stopping moment Uncle Richard and Stephen slipped again, but Stephen dug in.

"Can you shift your weight, Uncle Richard?" Stephen asked. "Give this rock behind us as much room as we can."

A torrent of stones ran down the ruined stairs while Stephen and Uncle Richard clung to each other, braced against the wall. One big chunk glanced off and hit Stephen's foot. He flinched, and they went sliding another yard or two, until he found a new point where he could brace himself. Finally the rock storm died down. Braced in the darkness of the tower, Stephen and Uncle Richard let loose shuddering sighs.

"It may sound silly, asking now," Stephen said, "but how did you get here? The last I saw you were on the train heading across the bridge."

"I was lucky," Uncle Richard said. "The train had to slow down when it crossed the bridge. Before it could speed up again I jumped off. Then I walked back over to the town. The whole population was busy looking at a big black car zooming away."

"That's the car *I* was in."

"So I guessed," Uncle Richard said. "I watched the car go up the cliff and head for the castle. Then I skirted the town and headed for this lovely pile myself. The front door is pretty heavily guarded."

"You don't have to tell me that," Stephen said.

"But there are sections where the walls have nearly fallen to the ground."

"Like that part right here."

"I climbed up to the battlements and was just starting to look around when I heard a commotion coming my way. Ducked into the guard tower, and you came running by."

While he talked Uncle Richard began picking his way down the steps. Stephen followed him. "I hope we won't meet anybody at the bottom of the stairs,'' he said.

"Not likely. Those fellows think you're dead. And they're the types who would be happy to leave you where you landed."

"But Mr. Fell might make them dig for us."

Uncle Richard stopped. "*Jonathan* Fell?"

Stephen nodded and told him what had happened after the fight.

"So, he wants me to do a job for him?" Uncle Richard murmured as he eased the tower door open. "Fat chance."

The tower opened into a tiny courtyard filled with broken paving stones and knee-high patches of grass. It reminded Stephen of a mangy animal.

There were no guards around, and a big gap in the wall stood conveniently close. Uncle Richard scouted the area, then tapped Stephen on the shoulder. "Move it!" he said. They dashed to the wall. Stephen pulled himself up onto a low section of the tumbled stone, but Uncle Richard was having trouble climbing up. His hands were scraped, and he had an ugly bruise on his wrist where the stone had hit him.

They made their way slowly over the wall and crept around to the front of the castle. "The old builders did us a favor here," Uncle Richard said, pointing down. "They cut a defensive ditch in the rock here. If we use it, the guards at the door won't notice us."

Bent over, they scuttled along. Stephen choked on the dust they raised. "This is hot!" he said.

"It could have been worse. Suppose they'd built a nice wet moat?"

The ditch had eroded away near the bridge. "Okay. A quick crawl across here, and we should be home free—as long as nobody is watching from the tops of those towers."

"What about the gate guards?" Stephen asked.

"It's out of their line of sight. Just be careful on the bridge. Trust me. I have a plan."

"The only thing you forgot is a getaway car," Stephen joked.

"We have one." Uncle Richard pointed to the ruins of the gatehouse at the far side of the bridge. Stephen saw that the ruins blocked the guards' view of a small path. Parked behind a broken wall was a battered, old cloth-topped Land-Rover. And standing beside it was a young woman with bright red hair.

Stephen turned to Uncle Richard. "Who's that?"

"Annie MacKenzie. She's a marine biologist. I met her on the way up here, by the Death Loch. She was taking samples, but she stopped what she was doing and agreed to help me."

Stephen's eyes narrowed.

"I wouldn't have gotten here so quickly if she hadn't given me a lift," Uncle Richard said, patting Stephen's arm.

Stephen shrugged. A ride was a ride, of course.

But leave it to Uncle Richard to find a pretty woman to do the driving.

They dashed across the bridge to the car.

Annie gave Stephen a warm smile when she saw him. "I thought your uncle was mad to come here alone, but I'm glad he got you back." She turned to Uncle Richard. "Did you have any problems?"

"I got into a bit of a scrape," Uncle Richard said, holding out his hands.

Annie reached into the Land-Rover and pulled out a small medicine chest. Taking out a bottle, she said, "I'm afraid this is going to hurt."

She poured a clear liquid onto Uncle Richard's scraped palms. Then she got busy wrapping bandages around them.

"Wonderful," Uncle Richard said. "Now let me get behind the wheel of that Rover and we'll move it out of here."

"I don't think that will be too easy," Annie said, embarrassed. Her bandage job had been more enthusiastic than expert. Uncle Richard looked as if he were wearing giant white mittens.

"This is ridiculous!" he said. "I can't do anything with these, including getting them off!" He struggled with the bandages.

Stephen turned away to keep from laughing, then jumped in horror as a set of claws raked the air beside his cheek.

"Kill him!" the raven shrieked, just missing his eyes. A length of broken chain dangled from its leg.

"One of Fell's pets!" Stephen yelled as the raven flew around for another pass. "It attacked me before."

The raven came down in a steep dive, aiming at Annie. She threw up an arm to protect herself. The bird reached for her hair, and flew away with a hank in its beak. "Maybe he likes redheads," Stephen said, feeling the draft from the bird's wings.

When the raven came diving again Uncle Richard stood ready on the hood of the Land-Rover. The bird dove at Annie once more, but one of Uncle Richard's white mittens smacked it off-course. The bird squawked and fluttered—then came straight at Uncle Richard. Blocked by the bandages, it tore at them with its claws and beak, crying, "Kill him! Kill him!" It ripped its way free, made for Annie, got hurled away again by Uncle Richard, and circled back. The bandages were in pretty sad shape, with new bloodstains on them. "We've got to trap it somehow," Uncle Richard said. "But what can we keep it in?"

"My testing case!" Annie dashed to the Land-Rover, grabbed a heavy canvas bag, and emptied it.

"Steve, take it. Annie, you'll have to be our bait."

She didn't much like the idea, but she stood her ground. The raven came diving at her again.

This time, instead of batting the bird away, Uncle Richard's mittened hands closed on its body as Annie ducked. The raven gave a great squawk of outrage and flapped its wings, trying to fly away. Uncle Richard grimly held on. The raven stabbed wildly with its beak at Uncle Richard while Stephen brought up the bag. The bird fought viciously, but Uncle Richard managed to bundle it in. Stephen zipped things up. The raven gave a muffled scream.

"I heard it! Musta flown over 'ere," a voice said from the other end of the ruins. Five guards with nets and blankets walked around the wall. They halted in astonishment when they saw the Land-Rover. "What the—" one of them said, going for his gun.

7

"YOU TAKE THE HIGH ROAD ..."

SATURDAY: 8:58 P.M., *Scotland*

Uncle Richard snatched the canvas bag from Stephen's hands and hurled it at the guard. Between the shock of getting hit and hearing the squawk that came from the bag, the man dropped his gun. Grabbing Annie, Uncle Richard shoved her behind the wheel of the Rover.

"Move it, Annie," Uncle Richard said. "These guys are killers. If we fall into their hands, we'll never come out alive."

She switched on the ignition, gunned the motor, and steered straight for the knot of men.

They scattered as the Land-Rover came roaring at them. Stephen saw one man yelling into a walkie-talkie.

The gates of the castle boomed open, and a fleet of

spanking-new Land-Rovers came zooming out, each loaded with men. Stephen counted nine cars.

A bullet whined past them. "Those guys are fast," Stephen said, ducking.

Annie took her Rover at top speed through the winding road that led from the bridge. "Where do we go now?" Uncle Richard asked.

"Back to Killy Bay?" Annie said.

"No," said Stephen. "The people there wouldn't help me when they saw me being kidnapped by four men. They certainly won't help us against ten times that number in Land-Rovers."

Uncle Richard looked back at their pursuers. "Fell must really have a hold on them."

The Land-Rovers sped down the road. "The villagers are terrified of Mr. Fell," Annie said. "Ever since the loch went dead they've had to pass under Raven Castle to go fishing out on the sea. Every morning Mr. Fell makes them stop their boats and doff their caps to the castle."

"How can he force them to do that?" Stephen yelled, then held on tight as the car went through a two-wheel turn.

"With a blast of machine-gun fire across their bows," Annie said. "I saw him do it to Harry MacGeachin's boat. Harry has had to talk soft since that." She shook her head. "When you're the man in the castle—with the police miles away from a remote little town—you can get away with a lot."

They reached a stretch of straight path running along the cliff.

"You've never had a run-in with Fell?" Uncle Richard asked.

"I'd like to see him try," Annie said, her green eyes flashing at Uncle Richard, then back to the road. "I came here as part of a Royal Commission to find out what's happened to the Death Loch. The others gave up—I suspect Fell had something to do with that—but I won't. Fell had best learn to watch his step around me."

Stephen turned around to see Fell's Land-Rovers catching up. "Can't you go any faster?" he asked.

"Not if we want to stay on the road," Annie responded, making the brakes squeal as she took a tight curve. "The big question is where should we go? Carrabash is the nearest town, but we're on the wrong side of the Death Loch. We'd have to go all the way around . . ."

". . . And Fell would have his bullies across by boat to cut us off." Uncle Richard finished Annie's sentence.

"Then our only hope is the cliff road to Dunbeath. It's a large town, and I don't believe Fell's hold extends that far." They screamed through another turn, then came to a fork in the road. Annie zoomed onto a dirt road that led them still higher onto the cliffs.

The first Land-Rover missed the fork altogether and went speeding down the other road. The second drove into the shower of gravel that sprayed up behind Annie's wheels and stopped.

"Shortcut," Annie said as the Rover whined upward. The dirt road was no more than a goat track, winding in and out between boulders and crags. "All Castle people use the long road. They don't know this one. It'll make them careful."

They heard a loud crash, then saw a plume of smoke rise behind them. "Ah. Well, he wasn't too careful, was he?" Annie grinned.

The path kept going up. Annie shifted gears, swerved around a rock outcrop, and drove the Land-Rover onto a wide, well-surfaced road.

"The cliff road, I take it," Uncle Richard said.

"It's the main route in the area," Annie said, flooring the gas pedal. "Which doesn't mean much." There wasn't a car to be seen in either direction along the road. "Not much traffic at this time of day— everyone should be home eating their dinners."

Stephen's stomach rumbled at the thought of food. "Sounds like a good idea. I'm starving," he said.

"Ah, we have a hungry man back there," Annie said as the car seemed to fly forward. "When we get to Dunbeath, I know a nice little inn. They'll fill you up with some good cullen skink."

"What's that?"

"Smoked fish, onions, milk, and potatoes—all cooked into a soup."

Stephen smiled politely at Annie in the rearview mirror.

She grinned back. "How about skirlies? Onion, oatmeal, and suet—fried together."

"And I thought Mom's health food was weird," Stephen said to Uncle Richard. He laughed.

But the grins left their faces after Annie checked the rearview miror. "Look behind you," she said. Six Land-Rovers came skidding after them onto the cliff road from the turnoff. The dirt path had given her a lead, however, and she fought to keep that edge.

"Another reason to take this road—there are very few straightaways," she said, rounding a sharp turn. The road lived up to its name, hanging on to the lip of the cliffs. Below them, the open sea boiled away at the cliff base, tossing up white clouds of spray. Chill air came in off the water. Stephen shivered.

The six cars behind them had spread out across the road. "They don't look too worried about anyone coming along," Uncle Richard muttered. He looked at his bandaged hands. "What I wouldn't give to be behind the wheel right now!"

Annie's nerve amazed Stephen. Whenever the line came up behind her, she veered back and forth, keeping them from getting ahead of her. They came up to a series of sharp turns. One of the Rovers zoomed up right on her tail and started ramming into her as she spun through the tight curves.

Her eyes flashed and her chin came up. "So that's the way of it, eh?" She eased up on the gas a bit, and the car slowed down. The rammer thought he saw his chance to get around her. He veered over, zooming between Annie's Land-Rover and the wall of the cliff.

"Hold tight now," Annie said. She gave a quick twist to the steering wheel. The Land-Rover slid over to sideswipe the front of the rammer's car. It bounced over to the cliff face. His front fender caught on the rock, and the car spun crazily around. The other Rovers had to jam on their brakes or make wild turns to avoid him. One piled into the Rover in the middle of the road; two others hit each other as they tried to steer clear of the wreck. "That should make them keep their distance," Annie said.

Stephen looked back at the confusion. It reminded him of one of the Smokey movies, with the cop cars all piling up. Stephen noticed one of the remaining Rovers had a whip aerial. "Is that guy driving with a CB, Uncle Richard?"

His uncle squinted back. "Can't be sure. But he is talking into a microphone. Watch out for surprises, Annie."

It came pretty quickly. They cleared a curve, only to find themselves streaking toward a pair of trucks parked across the road.

Annie's lips went white. She pumped the brakes, but even a Land-Rover isn't made to go from sixty to zero in nothing flat. They skidded back and forth across the road, brakes and tires screaming. Stephen closed his eyes.

Uncle Richard muttered, "Neat trick. Fell radioed for a roadblock."

There was no crash, so Stephen opened his eyes. The Rover's nose was only inches from the trucks. Men came running up toward them. Three Rovers came rounding the curve from behind them.

Still tight-lipped, Annie yanked the gearshift. The Rover roared off in reverse. Men scattered as the car picked up speed. Stephen felt a moment of hope. But how could they break through the line of Rovers which already had moved to block their path?

But Annie wasn't even looking at them. Her eyes were on the side of the road. The cliffs here had a gentler slope than those they had covered, but it was still too steep to drive on.

Annie ground the gears. "Get ready for a bumpy ride!" she yelled, and steered the car off the road. The Land-Rover bounced into a large furrow eroded in the cliffside.

The furrow opened into a narrow valley. "Glen Kessock," Annie announced as the car righted itself. "A lovely stream. Be thankful it's dry at this time of year."

They jounced their way along the empty stream bed. Stephen kept one hand on Uncle Richard's shoulder and the other clamped onto a roof support.

The car threw them back and forth as it hit rocks embedded in the ground. "Where will this take us?" Uncle Richard asked.

"Down to the moors," Annie answered. "This whole area is an ancient mountain valley. The sea flooded the old valley bottom—that's the loch. The sides of the old valley are now mountains and the cliffs. The bottom land that wasn't flooded is moorland. With luck, we'll leave these fellows there. But there is a bad side to it. . . ."

"What's that?" Stephen asked.

"Once we're down in the moors, we can't escape. All Fell will need is a few guards on the roads to the hills, and he'll have us."

The glen opened out, and the Land-Rover cut through purple heather. The incline was petering out. They heard crashing and banging behind them as the pursuing Rovers clattered down the glen.

"Persistent devils, aren't they?" Annie said, hauling on the wheel. The car made a broad turn and started heading out onto a wide, flat area. "We'll make for that stand of scrub pines and see what those others intend to do."

Only two Land-Rovers came bumping out of the glen. "Aha!" Annie said in amusement. "One must have broken down in a bad spot—holding up the whole parade."

But the hunters weren't giving up. Two Rovers came slewing around, still following doggedly. Annie's foot went flat to the floorboards as her Rover flew across the rolling moorland.

The other Rovers flew too, slowly overtaking their prey.

Stephen glanced at his watch. "It's getting pretty late," he said. "Won't we be able to lose them in the dark?"

"First time in Scotland?" Annie asked. "We're so far north, sundown won't come for hours yet."

Stephen found himself wishing time would fly. Then he wished he could fly—home. This short visit had moved way beyond Uncle Richard's schedule. He had the horrible suspicion that no matter how this ended, he'd be the late Stephen Lane—maybe in more ways than one.

When they reached the stand of stunted pines, Annie brought the car around in a half circle, and came out the other side of the trees—right into the path of one of the oncoming Rovers. "If we turn, they catch up with us," she said, leaning over the wheel. "So . . ."

She stomped hard on the gas pedal. Her Land-Rover shot forward, straight at the surprised driver of the other one.

Stephen clung to his hold on the support bar. "She's playing chicken with those guys! She's out of her mind!"

At the last moment Annie jerked the car to the left. Uncle Richard's mittened hand landed on her shoulder. "Right! Veer the car right!"

She zipped the car right across the nose of the enemy Land-Rover. The man in the seat beside the driver jerked around. A shot rang out. "Threw off

61

his aim,'' Uncle Richard said. "And didn't let him get a shot at the driver."

Annie's face was set in hard lines as she whirled the wheel around. Her Land-Rover skidded around sharply and rammed into the end of the Rover they had just missed. It flew forward to land with a crash among the trees. Her mouth was a tight line as she said, "One down."

The car skidded around again as the second Land-Rover came roaring up. Annie hunched over the wheel as she drove in a straight speed run. But the strain she had put on the Rover began to tell. The car wasn't moving as fast, and Stephen could smell something burning.

Their pursuer came drawing up to them on the left. And off to the right Stephen caught a flash of sunlight. "Is that a river over there?" he asked.

"Kessock Water," Annie said. "Can't let them catch us against it."

The other Rover was even with them now and beginning to pull ahead. Every time Annie tried evasive moves, she was cut off.

"This guy knows what he's doing," Uncle Richard said.

The ground now had a slight downward slope and was getting spongier. "Peat bog!" Annie cried. "If we get stuck here . . .."

She didn't need to say anything more.

They lost speed on the softer surface, but the

Land-Rover at their side kept pace with them. "He's waiting till we bog down," Stephen cried.

"Which can't be much longer," muttered Uncle Richard.

8

TORCHLIGHT MEETING

SATURDAY: 9:32 P.M., *Scotland*

Annie tossed her mane of red hair and stepped on the gas again. "Watch out!" she cried as the ground gave under their left wheels. The Land-Rover flipped over.

Stephen stifled a scream. The roof of the Rover squelched against the soggy earth, but the car kept rolling over. They were back upright in an instant, bouncing like mad—but on solid ground.

The other Land-Rover didn't come out so well. The driver had swerved to avoid a crash, running his car into a soft spot. It was bogged down to the tops of its tires. The men in the car piled out and ran toward Annie's Rover, but she was too quick for them. The motor roared back to life and the car pulled away.

"We've lost them," Annie said, "but where can we go? All the hill roads will be sealed off by now."

"Where will Fell least expect us to go?" Uncle Richard said. "Killy Bay!"

"I thought we said we shouldn't go there," Stephen said.

"With a bunch of goons after us, no." Uncle Richard smiled. "But, alone, maybe we'll get some answers about what's going on here." He turned to Annie. "How can we get there from here?"

"There's an old road around here someplace, and a bridge across Kessock Water. Beyond that the town is just minutes away."

"What are we waiting for?" Uncle Richard said. "Move it!"

The long purple twilight had fallen by the time they found the road. "The gloaming," Annie said. "Look how it softens the mountains. Isn't it beautiful?"

"It is indeed," Uncle Richard said, shifting in his seat to look at her.

Stephen shifted in his seat, too, and stared at Uncle Richard. "So what will we do when we get back to Killy Bay?"

Uncle Richard looked at him. "We don't really know what's going on," he said. "So there's no way we can plan what we're going to do."

"You mean you don't have any plan at all?" Stephen asked.

"We'll stop at the outskirts of town and decide

where to go from there. It shouldn't be hard. Killy Bay has the look of a classic quiet town."

Night was falling as they came over the hill overlooking the town. They saw lines of little whitewashed houses, some of them fallen into disrepair. But what really caught their eyes was the glow in the town square made by the light of dozens of torches.

"The roof of the old town hall fell in about a year ago," Annie said. "So now, when they have to have meetings, the people meet out in the square."

They coasted down so they wouldn't attract any attention. Annie parked her car behind one of the houses. "This is where I'm staying," she said. They walked past a little garden and blended into the rear of the crowd of villagers.

There was a statue in the middle of the square, and the speakers were standing in front of it. A man in a checked cloth cap spoke excitedly to the people. Stephen recognized him as the man who had wanted to help him at the train station.

"It nearly killed me today, watching them attack that man on the train, and dragging off that bairn . . ."

"You'd have been killed for sure if you'd tried to take a hand," a voice from the crowd called out. "That big Dougal wouldn't have left enough of you to make soup with."

"That's Harry MacGeachin up there," Annie whispered.

"I like what he's saying," Uncle Richard said.

"Harry, you called this meetin'. If you wanted to complain, it would have been just as easy to do it in the pub."

"I called this meeting because it's high time we talked about what's happening up in the castle instead of just complaining about it," Harry said. "It's not enough that Mr. Fell shoots at our fishing boats if we don't bow to his castle. It's not enough that he threatens to blast the cliffsides down and cut the loch off from the sea . . ."

"So that's what he's been holding over the villagers' heads," Annie said. "If they can't get out to sea, their fishing is gone."

"And a dying town becomes a ghost town," Uncle Richard said.

"There are strange doings up at the castle," Harry went on. "You've heard that Gillian MacCuish was sacked from her job there? Let her tell you why."

A young woman got up in front of the statue with Harry. "I was doin' the cleanin', and opened up one of the unused bedrooms—to give it a bit of a dust—but there was someone there, and he was tied to the bedstead!"

Uncle Richard ducked his head and called out, "What did he look like?"

"He was an old man," Gillian said, "with a big white beard."

68

"Hamish Claymore," Uncle Richard whispered. "So he does need help!"

Harry was talking again. "An auld man held prisoner—and now Fell's bully boys are dragging wee lads off the trains . . ."

I'm not such a wee lad, thought Stephen.

"Something rotten is going on up at the castle," Harry shouted.

"So what do you want to do, Harry, raise the clans?" Someone laughed in the crowd.

"He's a devil, he is. He'll kill the fishing here, and then what will we do?" another man cried.

"Who are we to say what should go on at the castle?" said a third man.

Annie's eyes glowed dangerously. "I've heard enough of this," she said, pushing her way through the crowd. She leaped up in front of the statue. "Listen to me!" she cried.

"It's Miss MacKenzie!"

Annie stood looking down at the crowd. The torchlight cast highlights in her red hair and sparkled in her eyes. "You're brave people, the sons and daughters of brave people. Years ago your people fought the English. Today you fight the sea for a living. So why are you so afraid to fight a tyrant?"

"He has guns," someone said.

"We have a few too!" Harry answered.

"Haven't you heard of the police?" Annie said. "If Fell is up to no good, he can be arrested—castle or no."

"We can't call the police," someone called out. "The telephone lines are dead."

"And someone pinched the radio—just before the train came in," another voice said.

"Fell is thorough. He wanted to make sure this place was cut off," Uncle Richard muttered.

"We can't even drive out," said someone else. "I see watchfires on all the roads to the hills."

"And you'll let all this go by?" Annie shouted. "What sort of Highlanders are you anyway!"

A murmur greeted those words.

"No one's ever beaten Fell!" someone cried out.

"Oh, no?" Annie beckoned to Uncle Richard, "Richard, come up here with Stephen."

The crowd parted around Uncle Richard and Stephen. "Strangers," the villagers muttered. "What are they doin' here?"

Uncle Richard and Stephen climbed up in front of the statue. "I don't suppose you got a good look at the man on the train," Annie said. "But here he is. Maybe you recognize the boy."

Harry leaned over to take a good look at Stephen. "It is! It is the lad!"

"His uncle here broke into the castle and rescued him. He's met Fell before . . . and beaten him too."

Murmurs rippled through the square as the crowd members eyed one another.

"But doesn't that mean Fell's men are out searching for you?" a voice boomed out over the shouting.

"He has dozens of men scouring the moors," Annie said. "And more are up guarding the roads against us."

Uncle Richard stood poker-faced, but Stephen knew that look. Wheels were turning inside that head. Suddenly his uncle began to speak. "What that means is fewer guards up at the castle."

The crowd was suddenly quiet, listening.

"If you want to get Fell, now is the time."

"But how?" someone yelled.

"I have a plan . . ." Uncle Richard said.

The villagers burst out in loud discussion when he outlined what he had in mind.

"You're mad!"

"You'll get yourself killed!"

"You'll get *us* killed!"

"The guards won't do anything if we have Fell in our hands," Uncle Richard said. "And if I can get into the castle again, I'll get him."

"That's a big if," Harry said.

"And what you're asking us to do—if you don't get him, it will be the end of us!" another villager said.

Harry shrugged. "As things look, we have only two choices—try this plan, and maybe face a quick end, or do nothing, and let Fell squeeze us to a slow, painful end."

"You blokes is wrong," a voice rang out over the square. "This whole plan is canceled—by us."

The voice didn't come from the crowd. It came from behind it. Everyone spun around. The speaker stood on a Land-Rover that had silently rolled into the town square. He sat back down in the driver's seat. Behind him, three men stood—leveling rifles into the crowd.

9

A DANGEROUS GAME

SATURDAY: 10:50 P.M., *Scotland*

Stephen could feel the sullen silence that filled the town square—and the fear lying under it. The man in the driver's seat didn't seem to notice anything.

"Thought we wouldn't come looking down here, mate?" he said to Uncle Richard. "Wrong-o. The guv'nor sent us here first thing—after we got untangled from that mess you made up on the cliff road." He shot a dirty look at Annie, then jerked his hand in a curt come-on gesture.

"I got my orders. Yer to come up to the castle, all three. You, the brat, and the girl. Hop it!"

Stephen and Annie started moving forward. Uncle Richard quietly grabbed hold of their belts and stopped them.

The driver shouted. "Now! 'Op it!"

"Lost your *H* there," Uncle Richard shouted back.

It didn't make the driver any friendlier. His lips tightened. "Awright, sport. *Hhhhhop it!* Happy now? So get your dainty toes over here!"

Uncle Richard just smiled at him. The villagers began to move away.

No shots came. Fell's bully boys had come prepared for anything but this. One of the riflemen hoarsely whispered to the driver, "What do we do now, Bert?"

Bert's answer was to rip a pistol from his holster and point it at Uncle Richard. "You coming? Or do I have to pop a few into yer?"

The smile on Uncle Richard's face only broadened in answer, even as the barrel of the pistol came up to cover him. "Did Mr. Fell tell you to pop a few into me? I thought he wanted me to work for him."

Bert glared over his pistol. "Keep it up, sport. I might just forget about what Mr. Fell told me."

Uncle Richard kept smiling. "I wouldn't be surprised. You look like the type who'd have trouble keeping two thoughts in his head at the same time."

A nervous giggle went through the crowd. Bert heard it, and his face flamed. "Look, Yank, I'm gettin' tired of playin' with you. Are you coming along?"

Uncle Richard leaned back against the statue. "I

don't think so.'' He gave a negligent glance at Bert's pistol. ''Now, why don't you put your courage away before it goes off and hurts you?''

Stephen watched the pistol shake as Bert's hand quivered with rage. If the gun went off now, nobody could tell who the target would be.

''You—'' Bert choked out.

Uncle Richard threw his arms wide open. ''Go ahead! Shoot me! Have fun. My only regret is that I won't be there when you explain it to Fell. 'Well, yer see, Guv, it were this way . . . I 'ad to shoot 'im. 'E was callin' me names . . .' ''

Stephen couldn't figure out what Uncle Richard was trying to do. Get killed? If only Uncle Richard had a gun! ''Guns are sometimes useful on adventures, but impossible to get past airport security these days,'' his uncle had once explained. ''If I can pick one up where I'm going, fine. But I'd be a fool to carry one.'' Maybe Uncle Richard was right. Bert was carrying a gun, and right now he looked like a fool, steaming behind the wheel of his Land-Rover.

Finally he rammed his pistol back into his holster. ''Jimmy! Fred! Smudger!'' he barked to the three riflemen behind him. ''Foller me!''

''Bert, we ain't supposed to shoot 'im,'' one of the men said as he hopped down from the Land-Rover.

''Fell didn't say nothin' about not markin' him up a little,'' Bert snarled. ''We'll see how smart his mouth is after I hammer his mug a bit.''

Stephen could feel the tension building as Fell's men started to push their way through the crowd. The people glared at Fell's men. They didn't give way as the men pushed forward. Little ripples of muttering swept through the villagers as they jostled about. Uncle Richard leaned forward a little, tensing himself.

"I've got to hand it to you, Bert, you've got plenty of guts." Uncle Richard's voice cut across the crowd.

"Wotcher mean, sport?" Bert said.

"Walking into the middle of a crowd like this— with only three men . . ."

For a moment everything froze. The silence was electric. Then the villagers surged like a wave over Bert and his buddies. One rifle went off into the air. The noise was drowned out by the roar of the crowd. Fists flew for a moment, then an open spot appeared. Harry MacGeachin stood in the middle of it. "No killing!" he yelled. At his feet were Bert and the other guards, out cold.

"You suckered those guys into that!" Stephen said, amazed.

"That was a dangerous game," Annie said. "You suckered the people in as well."

As the excitement died down, the townspeople realized it too. It got very quiet.

Harry McGeachin spoke up loudly. "Well, if you're going to try this crazy plan, you can use my boat." He looked from the guards to his neighbors. "In for a penny, in for a pound."

The crowd actually laughed at that. "What have we got to lose?" one man yelled.

Silence fell. Nobody wanted to answer that question.

10

DEEP WATERS

SATURDAY: 11:19 P.M., *Scotland*

Moments later they were on the dock, standing by Harry's boat—a forty-foot trawler. "She's a good machine," Harry said, patting the side rail. "Gone many a long mile in her."

"How about showing us our course, Harry?" Uncle Richard said.

They climbed aboard and went aft to the wheelhouse. Harry unrolled a chart. He pointed at a long finger of blue pushing its way from the sea into the mountains. "This is Loch Killy. We call it a sea loch because it connects with the sea." His face went grim. "Or the Death Loch, as many people call it these days."

He brought his finger halfway along the loch. "Here is Killy Bay." The finger moved on. "And here, right at the point where the loch joins the sea, is Raven Castle.'' His finger stabbed at a headland jutting out into the blue, nearly cutting the sea off from the loch.

''Our course will take us from the town to Crag Mor.'' He pointed at a little dot near the castle.

''What does that mean?'' Stephen asked.

''It's Gaelic for Big Rock,'' Annie said.

''What is it?''

''A big rock sticking up in the middle of the loch,'' Harry said. ''It will hide us from the castle.''

''Will they be looking for us?''

''No, but they could hear our engine. Sound carries across the water.'' Uncle Richard turned to Harry. ''What do we do next?''

''From Crag Mor to the headland we let the tide take us. The engine will be cut off, so the castle people shouldn't hear us coming.'' Harry cleared his throat. ''Then we come to the ticklish part, bringing the boat close to the shore and getting you onto the land.''

Stephen had visions of the boat helplessly tossed against the rocky cliffs, smashing itself into toothpicks. Maybe they should think of another way to get into the castle. But it was too late. Harry had already started the engine. Uncle Richard cast off the lines, and they headed out into the loch.

The floorboards of the wheelhouse vibrated from the engine, and the whole boat rocked on the swell of the waves. Harry stood at ease behind the wheel, his cap pushed back on his head. He squinted into the darkness ahead.

They reached deep water soon. The swells became higher, and Stephen had a moment of queasiness. He distracted himself by working the buttons on his watch. First an arrowhead appeared on the dial. "We're heading north-northwest," he said.

Uncle Richard looked at his watch and nodded. "Now check the echo ranger," he said. More buttons. This time, words appeared on the dial. *Obstruction . . . 20 feet . . . dead ahead.*

"Hey," Stephen said. But the boat was stopping. He could hear waves breaking.

Crag Mor lived up to its name. It was a black needle of rock jutting out of the water. "Can't get too close," Harry said.

They stood off from the rock for a few moments more, then the moon rose from behind Castle Head, silhouetting the headland and the gaunt wreckage of the old castle.

"Certainly enough holes in those walls to get us in," Uncle Richard said. "The only problem is getting up to them."

"There's a shelf of rock I can leave you at—it's the beginning of a sort of path. That's really too strong a name for it. It's a climbing way that I and a few others used when we were lads. It was our castle then, before Mr. Fell came with his London money and rapid-fire guns." Harry's look at the castle was a mixture of regret for a lost youth and hatred for the man who now lived there. "We'll wait a few minutes to see if we'll get a bit of mist to hide our movements."

Harry was a good prophet. A light fog rolled in from the sea. It made the castle seem unreal. Stephen hoped it made the boat seem just as unreal to anybody looking down from the castle walls.

They took a few minutes to eat some sandwiches that Harry had brought along. Annie found Harry's first-aid kit and rebandaged Uncle Richard's hands. He was happy to get rid of the big mittens. But Stephen noticed that he looked worriedly at his injured wrist.

The boat bobbed along on the tide, its engine silent. Harry stood a little straighter at the wheel, steering carefully. The cliffs came closer, growing until the mass of rock frowned down over them. A white line of waves broke all along the bottom of the headland.

They swept along, silent except for the slapping of waves against the hull, nearing the rocks. Harry pointed ahead. There was a big flat rock about the size of a dinner table. Most of the time it stood above the water. Making tiny corrections on the wheel, he steered them toward it. They left him in the wheelhouse, and went out onto the deck.

The boat moved smoothly past the rock. Uncle Richard jumped, and landed on the flat space. He turned and opened his arms, and Stephen jumped. Annie followed.

They stood and waved good-bye to Harry, flowing

81

with the tide out to sea. When he was some distance from the castle, he'd turn on the engine again. Then, hugging the opposite side of the loch entrance, he'd make his way back to Killy Bay and lead the villagers by land to the castle.

"That will be the last friendly face we see for a while," Uncle Richard said quietly. Stephen looked up the grooved slope of the headland. From where they stood, only a tiny bit of the castle was visible. "It may be the last friendly face we ever see."

11

THE CRACK IN THE CASTLE WALL

SUNDAY: 12:26 A.M., *Scotland*

Fed and rested as they were, the trip up the cliff should have been a snap. Generations of little boys from Killy Bay had almost worn a path to the top. Still, Stephen worried every step of the way, watching how awkwardly Uncle Richard climbed. The wrist injured by the rock on the tower stairs was weak, and it slowed him.

Several times Stephen gritted his teeth, watching his uncle make dangerous moves just to keep up. Would Uncle Richard be able to keep up if they had to make a fast escape?

He rested on the stony slope for a moment, waiting for Uncle Richard to come up. Annie was way ahead of them both.

Uncle Richard came clambering up a grooved furrow

that in rainy weather must have been a fast-flowing spring. When he saw Stephen he stopped in surprise. "Tired?" he asked. Stephen looked at his uncle's wrist. "Are you sure we should be doing this?" he whispered.

"We have no choice. Either we get Fell, or he gets us. There's just no time for anything else." Uncle Richard stifled a curse as he missed a handhold. "We've got to move it—bad wrist and all."

Run-off springs had gouged deep furrows in the sides of the headland, and made natural paths to the flat space where the castle stood. Soon they stood at the head of one of these little valleys, looking up at the castle walls. Only the tall main section showed signs of life, light shining out of the windows. But here and there along the walls, specks of light gave away guard posts.

"Very careless, letting the guards use their flashlights on patrol," Uncle Richard said. "Tells us just where they are."

Silently he led the way across the rocky tableland. The rugged ground was perfect for sneaking around. Cuts in the ground, boulders thrusting up, and piles of stonework fallen from the walls gave them their choice of hiding places.

Even the moonlight was on their side, casting odd shadows on the ground. Often they would hear guards shouting at nonexistent intruders, shining their flashlights on suspicious-looking rocks.

"They seem nervous tonight," Annie whispered.

"Their kind is always happiest in large packs," Uncle Richard answered. "And most of their friends are scattered around the valley, looking for us."

He led them up to the bottom of the castle walls. "I noticed a break in the wall up ahead here."

Abruptly he froze in the shadows, motioning Annie and Stephen to lie flat. Over their heads a flashlight beam cut the air. "I tell you, I saw something move in that hole in the wall over there," a voice said.

"The thing's ten feet off the ground. You'll drive me mad, you will," another voice answered.

They listened as the argument moved away from the section of wall and out into a courtyard beyond it.

"Guards patrolling the inside of the ruins too," Uncle Richard murmured. "This makes things a bit more difficult."

They continued moving, skirting the wall. Whenever they found a section where the wall had collapsed, they also saw the beams of flashlights inside the ruins.

"Keep up at this, and we'll make a grand circle around the castle," Annie said.

Uncle Richard went a few more steps ahead. "Stop," he whispered. "Look at this."

Some blocks had shaken loose from a cracked wall, leaving a narrow V-shaped opening. The remaining blocks made a rough staircase up to the battlements.

"Wonderful," Stephen muttered. "Another climb." But the ascent went quickly enough. They had almost reached the top when a stone slipped beneath Annie's foot. She recovered herself quickly, but the rock went sailing down into the darkness, landing with a huge crash.

"What's that?" said a voice above them on the battlements. "We should go and take a look." Stephen, Annie, and Uncle Richard froze.

We're like sitting ducks stuck on this wall, Stephen thought.

"Ye're daft," another voice came out of the dark. "It's just another bleeding rock falling. They fall all the time around this barn. So quitcher jumping."

"I know that voice," Stephen whispered to Uncle Richard. "It's my old friend, Foxy-face. What's his real name?"

"I'm sorry, Davey," the first voice came back. "I don't like it here. It's cold . . ."

"We should be happy to be alive after what happened today. Mr. Fell was *not* happy to hear that geezer wasn't in Carrabash. Cor! The look he gave me . . . And it's all your fault! You were supposed to do him on the train, then bring him here!"

" 'E 'it me, Davey. I didn't expect that." Dougal sounded apologetic.

" 'E 'it me," Davey mimicked. "I'll give you a conk, too, you great twit!" There was a thump, and a muttered "Ooooh!"

Uncle Richard had to smother a laugh.

"They really are like a criminal Laurel and Hardy," Stephen muttered. "But how can we get rid of them?"

"I shoulda snuffed him, that's what I shoulda done," Dougal said. "Choked the life outa him, the way you said. Then there would have been no problems."

"Except with Mr. Fell, you mean," Davey shot back. "He wants him to go diving in the loch, after that stuff down there."

"I could kill him, and they could blast it loose," Dougal said stubbornly.

"They could blast at yer 'ead, once you get an idea stuck," Davey snapped. "Any sort of explosion destroys the stuff. I dunno how it came through when the sub sank. . . ."

"What is this sub nonsense?" Stephen whispered. He turned to Uncle Richard. But his uncle had that "wheels-turning" look on his face. He crept up almost to the level of the battlements, then pried one of the stones loose and hurled it down into the dark. It landed with a satisfying crash.

"There it goes again," Dougal said.

"Yer a case, you are. That madman nobody knows where, the brat on the loose, and people helping him escape—especially that MacKenzie woman—and you carry on about rocks falling. Well, I'll make you happy. I'll take a dekko." Davey's flashlight beam came close to the edge of the crack. "I don't see nothing," he said. "Nothing at all." Uncle Richard's hand snaked up to grab Davey's foot, and tugged.

"Arragh!" Davey yelled, toppling backward. His head landed with a *thunk!*

"Davey! Davey! What's happened to you?" Dougal came rushing up, his flashlight casting a wildly bobbing beam. "Cor! What have they done to you?" he whimpered.

Uncle Richard heaved himself onto the top of the wall, with Stephen and Annie right behind him. For a brief moment the moon came out, throwing their shadows across Davey as Dougal knelt over him. Before the big man could get to his feet, Uncle Richard was behind him, a rock in his hand. It caught Dougal on the back of his head. He slumped right beside Davey.

Uncle Richard knelt by the unconscious pair and started going through their pockets. "What are you doing?" Annie whispered.

"Looking for something," Uncle Richard answered. "Ah . . . I was right." Out of Davey's coat came a big pistol and some ammunition. Uncle Richard looked grimly at Annie. "I'm afraid I'm going to need this."

12

"I'LL TAKE THE LOW ROAD ..."

SUNDAY: 1:33 A.M., Scotland

They found a guard tower conveniently nearby, with a crumbling doorway where they could store Dougal and Davey. Uncle Richard tumbled them in, then the three of them ran along the battlements. "Quick, we don't want a run-in with another patrol," Uncle Richard said.

The footing on the walkway was treacherous—shadows looked like holes, and holes looked like shadows. Sometimes they had to duck into doorways to hide from passing guards. Stephen began to enjoy it—like playing hide-and-seek.

They had crept up to the wall of a major tower just as a pair of guards came walking along the courtyard below. Stephen spied a doorway to his left and ducked into it. His right foot landed on stone, his left foot on air. For a long moment he teetered on a tiny stone ledge, all that was left of a long-lost floor.

Stephen grabbed the doorframe and clung with a death grip, eyes closed. A light breeze ruffled his clothes. In his position it was almost enough to send him over.

After an eternity Uncle Richard and Annie appeared from the hiding places they had used while the guards patrolled below. Uncle Richard hauled Stephen to safety. "An important rule in the adventuring game, Steve," he said. "When you jump through a door, make sure there's a floor."

"There was," Stephen said. "Only it was four stories down."

"When you've finished your chat, maybe you could tell me something. How do you plan to get into the live part of the castle?" Annie said.

From his vantage point on the wall Uncle Richard looked over the main courtyard. Once it had been a garden, and plots of trees and bushes still survived. Beyond them rose the bulk of the main building, windows glowing with light. "The front door will be crawling with guards," he said. "So we'll get in by following our noses."

"Can I have that again?" Stephen said.

"Take a deep breath," Uncle Richard suggested.

Stephen and Annie did as he said.

"What do you smell?"

There was a salty tang from the water, the musty smell of moss on stone, the smell of trees and plants,

and beneath that, a sort of unpleasant stink. It reminded Stephen of a summer day when the local garbage cans hadn't been emptied. He turned to Uncle Richard. "Garbage?" he asked.

His uncle grinned. "Got it. Fell considers himself a gentleman. He'd never have the garbage going and coming through the door he uses. No, if I know him, all garbage goes out through the kitchen door, which has to be in the back of this big pile. And since it's protected by the back wall, and all these guards, I'll bet nobody is watching it."

They worked their way down into the courtyard, sniffing all the way. Sure enough, the smell of garbage got stronger. "Gad, this is disgusting," Annie said.

"It is pretty ripe," Uncle Richard said. "I expect it's supposed to be dumped quite often, but the servants goof off. If Fell knew, he would probably go into a rage—fire his butler, or whatever."

Beyond a little stand of trees stood a collection of cast-iron cans filled with trash.

"Well, we've found it," Annie said. "What next?"

"Over there," Uncle Richard said. Stephen couldn't see anything. "We'll risk a light." Uncle Richard pointed his watch. A thin, brilliant beam shot out, illuminating an old, roughly made door.

"Kitchen entrance," Uncle Richard said.

"Lead on, Mighty Smeller," Annie said.

Uncle Richard hesitated, reaching into his jacket for his pistol. He led them to the door, and grasped the knob. It turned in his hand.

A moment later they were in the castle, sneaking along a corridor past the kitchen. No need to tiptoe. The clanging and banging of pots and pans covered any noise they made. Even the kitchen entrance was easy, thanks to a falling stack of plates. "You cack-handed idjit!" the cook yelled, drawing everyone's attention while Stephen, Uncle Richard, and Annie sneaked by.

They tiptoed down a corridor, meeting no one. It ended finally in a big oak door soundproofed with green material. "End of servants' territory—the house is on the other side," Stephen said.

"How do you know that?" Annie said.

"I watched *Upstairs, Downstairs* on TV," Stephen said.

He was right. The great hall of the castle was on the other side of the door—Fell's bizarre Hall of Weapons. "I can see his business is still booming," Uncle Richard whispered.

"He said he'll make money as long as people keep fighting—and need guns to fight," Stephen said.

Annie's lip curled. "Sounds like a real charmer, he does."

Uncle Richard kept close to the wall of the hall, checking out the exits. "You remember where they took you?" he asked Stephen.

"We went down that corridor to the left of the fireplace. Next came a big door, then the stairs."

"Any other doorways off the stairs?"

"No, I don't think so. I don't remembering seeing any."

"That leaves three other corridors to try. How about the one nearest us?" He eased open the door. Drifting down the hallway came the sounds of a card game and the smell of beer. Uncle Richard closed the door. "Troop quarters. I'd recognize them anywhere."

The next door looked a lot more promising. It opened on a stairway, and they followed it up. Some of the landings were dusty. It was clear they hadn't been used in a while. "Nobody here," Uncle Richard said, going on. They finally came up to a hall with a splendid Oriental rug on the floor and crystal lamps on the walls. "Aha. Fell territory. Careful now . . ."

He crept along the hall, opening doors as he went. They were all bedrooms. Most of them looked disordered, as if they had been left in a hurry. "Fell's officers—called to duty when you escaped," Uncle Richard said.

Behind one door they found a large bedroom with a big four-poster in it. Dangling from one of the posts was a set of handcuffs. "Remember what Gillian what's-her-name said? She saw an old man tied to the bedstead." Uncle Richard flipped the handcuffs. "Well, Hamish isn't here any longer. They left one set of handcuffs here and used the other set—"

"How do you know there were two?" Annie said.

"The scratches on the other bedpost. They kept him here with two sets of handcuffs, and used one set to take him away. Where?'' He left the room, heading for the last room on the floor.

It was Fell's bedroom, and it was empty. Standing in the door made Stephen feel like a Peeping Tom. The room was filled with expensive furniture, silk wallpaper, silk covers on the bed, and all sorts of military hardware. ''Fell always had a thing for weapons,'' Uncle Richard said. He looked at a painting on the wall—soldiers being blown up by an exploding shell. ''He has weird taste in art too.''

Uncle Richard searched the room carefully. He found a concealed safe, several pistols hidden around the room, and nothing else. He even nosed the drapes aside with his gun, but didn't find his friend Hamish —or Fell.

''Well, we've gone up and haven't found anything. That leaves only one direction—down.'' He headed back to the stairs. ''I'm sure a place like this would have a dungeon . . .''

The entrance to the castle dungeon was down the one hallway they hadn't tried from the great hall. It led to another spiral staircase, this one in better repair. The walls became clammier as they went down. Uncle Richard turned to Annie and Stephen, raising a finger to his lips. Suddenly he stopped, and motioned them to back up.

''There's a guard at the door,'' he whispered when they were out of earshot. ''We need a distraction.

Annie, do you want to use your feminine wiles on him?''

"I find that demeaning," she said.

Uncle Richard shrugged. "Just an idea. That leaves you, Steve."

"I think I liked the feminine wiles better," Stephen muttered.

"All you have to do is keep this guy looking at you for a moment . . . so I can get down the stairs and jump him."

A few seconds later Stephen came walking down the stairs and right up to the guard at the dungeon door. It was the same one who had stood outside his cell. "Hi, there," Stephen said. "I understand Mr. Fell is looking for me."

The man gawked at him. He never saw Uncle Richard come down the last spiral of the stair and leap on him.

It wasn't even a struggle. Uncle Richard soon laid him out. "That was pretty good, Steve," he grinned.

Stephen took his trembling hands out of his pockets. "I didn't know what else to say."

Uncle Richard's face became serious again. He pulled his gun out. "No place left in the castle. Hamish and Fell must be in there. Problem is, we don't know who else might be around. I'm going in first. If there's no shooting, you and Annie come in after me. Let's move it." He kicked the door open.

It wasn't exactly a dungeon inside. In fact, it

reminded Stephen of the big command post in *Dr. No*. A large radio set covered a work table, and a bank of TV monitors stood behind it. On one wall was a map of the valley with areas marked off. Jonathan Fell was sticking pins into the map. He whirled around, dropping a box of colored pins. The sudden movement set off a startled squawk from the raven chained to a metal perch.

They were alone in the room, except for Hamish Claymore, an elderly man with powerful shouders. He must have been an impressive specimen when he worked for British Intelligence. Now he sat hunched over, handcuffed to a wooden chair, his hair and beard unkempt, eyes sunk deep in his head. For the first time in a long time hope seemed to gleam in them.

"You miserable . . ." Uncle Richard said. "Forcing him to watch while you conducted the search, eh?" His gun centered rock-steady on Fell.

"The poor man!" Annie cried when she saw Hamish. She rushed into the room to help him, dashing right in front of Uncle Richard.

"Don't block him—" Stephen yelled, but it was too late.

Annie never got near Hamish. Fell's cane flipped between her legs and she tripped, hitting the floor hard. As she landed, a gun popped into Fell's hand. It was aimed right at her head.

The raven fluttered madly around its perch in

excitement. Fell allowed himself a crooked grin as he looked down at Annie's shocked face. "Duffy, I suggest you put that pistol down. Otherwise I'll have to dye this young lady's hair quite another shade of red."

13

HIGH-PRESSURE DIVING

SUNDAY: 2:08 A.M., *Scotland*

Uncle Richard's gun clattered on the stone floor. Fell pulled it over with his cane. He spent a moment calming down his pet raven. Then he called out the open door. "Oswald, are you feeling fit enough to come in and join us?"

A gurgle came from outside, then the guard came walking in stiffly.

"Oswald is my bodyguard. He always stays close to me. A good man, Oswald is." Fell gave them his marble-toothed smile.

At that point the one thing Oswald looked least like was a good man. He had a bruise on his forehead, a snarl on his lips, and big gun in his hand. If Fell told him to make us look like Swiss cheese, he'd think it was Christmas, Stephen thought.

All at once the bank of video monitors behind Fell lit up. Several showed different views of the area just beyond the drawbridge into the castle. Little pinpoints of light danced in the distance. Torches.

Fell went to the controls. "You'd find my security system quite interesting, Duffy," he said. "TV cameras with telescopic lenses, long-distance microphones . . ."

The pictures became sharper. They could see the villagers clutching old hunting rifles, pistols, and even a couple of old swords. One monitor gave a close-up of Harry MacGeachin marching in the lead.

Fell turned to look at Uncle Richard. "You've been very busy rabble-rousing," he said. "Not that it worries me. I learned long ago that the way to stop a rebellion is to cut off the head." He gave them a bow. "And I believe in this case the head is you and Miss McKenzie here. Why don't you get up off the floor, my dear. Slowly, of course." Fell turned back to the monitor to sneer at Harry MacGeachin. "That stupid fisherman couldn't lead his way out of a paper sack."

He picked up the microphone from his radio set. "Tower guards?" he called.

A staticky voice answered. "East tower guards. Yes, Mr. Fell."

Another voice came in. "West tower guards reporting, sir."

Fell smiled. "The monitors show a large group of

hostiles advancing on the bridge,'' he said. ''Unlimber the machine guns.''

He turned to the people in the room. ''They're set up to lay down a crossfire around that bridge.'' Then he spoke into the microphone again. ''When they get to the bridge, turn on your searchlights. Then patch me into your loudspeaker systems.'' He cackled, sending chills through Stephen.

The villagers marched along on the monitors, waving their torches, confident of winning the good fight. Then the searchlights lanced down from the towers, flooding the bridge area with harsh white light. The villagers froze, half-blinded, like insects caught on a tablecloth.

Fell spoke into his microphone, and Stephen could hear his voice boom out over bullhorns in the towers. ''Put down your weapons. Stand where you are.''

Shouts came up from the villagers, but the loudspeaker drowned them out. ''This is your last warning. Put the guns—and whatever else you have—down.''

More pictures of the villagers appeared on the monitors. Stephen got a better view of the village arsenal. Some carried pitchforks, and one old man had a ten-foot-long pike on his shoulder. They shook their weapons defiantly.

''If you won't surrender, you'll have to take the consequences.'' Fell's voice sounded brassy over the loudspeakers. ''Plan A,'' Fell said. He put a hand over the microphone and spoke to the people in the room. "Just warning shots."

The responses came immediately. "East tower. Understood."

"West tower. Understood." Behind the voices came clacking sounds—the noises of the machine guns being prepared for firing.

Then tongues of flame flashed over the battlements to the quick hammering of rapid fire. Two lines of holes stitched into the earth in front and behind the crowd. The angry yells stopped as the villagers drew together in a little knot.

They tried to run from their exposed spot back to the sheltering rocks at the neck of the headland. A storm of lead from the machine guns tore up the ground ahead of them. That stopped them cold.

"You are not to leave the area," Fell's voice blared. "Drop your weapons and stand where you are."

A villager raised his rifle to his shoulder, aiming for one of the searchlights.

Fell's amplified voice roared out. "Any firing from you will provoke counterfire from us. I warn you, we will exterminate you."

The man put his rifle down. A microphone near the group picked up his words. "Harry," he said, "what are we goin' to do?"

A close-up showed Harry MacGeachin's face; it was the picture of despair. His torches put to shame by the castle's floodlights, his shouts drowned out by the loudspeakers, his weapons put to scorn by the display of firepower—Fell had won it all.

"Is your new coat bulletproof, Harry, that ye think ye can lead us against machine guns?" one of the villagers cried out.

Fell turned from the monitors to face Uncle Richard. "Are you now willing to take care of the job I wanted you to do?" he asked. "Or do we find out about Harry's coat?"

"He's bluffing," Annie shouted. "Massacre all those people? He'd never get away with it."

The raucous voice of the raven suddenly rang out. "Kill them! Kill them!" it shrieked. It shocked everyone into momentary silence. Stephen's eyes flicked from the bird to Fell's microphone to the screens. He had a vivid picture of the tower guards taking the raven's words as an order.

But the situation outside hadn't changed. Uncle Richard glanced from the bird to Annie. "Maybe he's just crazy enough to try it." Then he looked at Fell for a long moment. "Doesn't look like I really have a choice."

"You have intelligence at least," Fell said. He motioned for Oswald to free Hamish from the wooden chair. "Of course, given the circumstances, I'll have to insist that you get to work immediately. Can't keep those villagers out on the bridge forever."

He opened a door on the far wall of the command

post. A dank breeze wafted into the room. "You'll go first, old man. This corridor leads straight to where we want to go."

Supporting Hamish, Uncle Richard started down the hallway. Annie and Stephen followed. Then came Fell and Oswald, guns at the ready.

The hallway became a tunnel and angled down into the ground. They could hear a roaring sound in the distance, and moments later found themselves standing in a white concrete cavelike room opening onto the loch.

"This was originally built as an escape route, but the constant banging of the tides wore most of it away," Fell said. "The secret underwater entrance and most of the loch end of the tunnel were lost. I rebuilt it as my diving room."

He looked at Uncle Richard. "Well, don't stand there, select your equipment. You'll find the newest protective suits and a good supply of air tanks."

Uncle Richard looked over the diving gear hanging on the walls, and selected a suit, tanks, mask, and an underwater flashlight. "How about a knife?" he said.

Fell looked amused. "Do you expect to meet the Death Loch monster? Nothing lives down there. You have no need for a knife." He nodded. "Nice try though."

"How about tools?"

"You might need them. Oswald will open the tool

locker and show you where to change. Go ahead," he said to his bodyguard. "I can take care of things here." Stephen watched his uncle march off with Oswald at his back. For a moment he looked at Fell, nursing wild schemes for jumping him and getting his gun.

Fell gave him another marble smile. "You're a brighter boy than I thought, getting out of your cell." He gestured with his pistol. "Don't go ruining my good opinion of you by doing something foolish now." Stephen slumped back.

It wasn't long before Uncle Richard returned, suited up. "Where am I going?" he asked.

"Into the loch of course—you know that much." Fell took a waterproof chart out of his tweed jacket. Your final destination is marked here. It's a submarine —vintage World War II."

Uncle Richard merely raised his eyebrows. "And?"

"There's a break in the hull, as this photograph shows." Fell tossed the picture to Uncle Richard. "You're to enter the sub, find the captain's quarters, and salvage a set of metal canisters. I don't know how many there are, but I suspect that at least one of them has broken open."

"What's in the canister?" Uncle Richard said.

Fell smiled slyly. "That would be telling."

"You have divers of your own. Why couldn't they do this job for you?"

"They aren't as familiar with—shall I say, dangerous

—environments as you are.'' Fell looked sour. ''They wouldn't go—all of them afraid, the miserable cowards. But I remembered you. With your training you should be able to do the job. Since you're retired, no one would miss you much. And if you fail, *I* certainly wouldn't miss you.'' Fell's eyes glittered.

That's his whole reason, Stephen thought. He'd be as happy to see Uncle Richard die as he would to have him carry the job off.

Uncle Richard stood with his diving mask in his hand, staring at Fell. Then with his eyes still locked on the old man's, he spat on the faceplate.

Fell jerked for a second, then sneered. ''French prisoners used to spit before going to the guillotine—to show their mouths weren't dry with fear.''

Uncle Richard flashed him a grin. ''Keeps the faceplate from misting up.'' His grin got wider. ''Of course, it didn't hurt that I was looking at you.''

Fell's face was white with rage. ''Get diving!'' His voice rose and he aimed his gun at Uncle Richard.

''That's hardly an incentive, Jonathan,'' Uncle Richard said.

Fell's eyes snapped shut. ''You've pushed me far enough. I'll give you an incentive.'' He pointed at the equipment. ''There's a diver's propulsion vehicle in here, and a cargo net. Use them to get to the sub, and recover those canisters within twenty minutes, or your three charming friends here will die.''

Both Fell's pistol and Oswald's covered Uncle

Richard. He glared at them for a minute, then pulled the helmet over his head. Digging through a pile of equipment, he grasped one of the handles on the torpedo-shaped propulsion jet. He pulled it free and walked to the water's edge.

"Your time starts . . . NOW!" the old man called after him.

Uncle Richard dropped into the water.

14

THE VILLAIN'S TALE

SUNDAY: 2:29 A.M., *Scotland*

Fell made his way to another bank of video monitors and sat down in front of them, keeping one eye on his prisoners. "More security," he said, flipping switches. Stephen saw an eerie greenish glow fill the loch waters outside the mouth of the cave.

"Underwater lighting." Fell continued working at the control console. The monitors popped to life. "Underwater cameras too." He made the cameras scan about, until one screen caught a tiny figure jetting along behind the propulsion unit—Uncle Richard. It reminded Stephen of the underwater sequences from a movie he had seen. But would Uncle Richard escape the danger the way James Bond had?

Stopping for a moment, Uncle Richard checked

the waterproof chart, then continued on. Several cameras caught him now from different distances and angles.

Fell punched more buttons. New monitors came on, featuring the wrecked shark-shape of a submarine. Stephen had expected it to be covered with seaweed and muck after forty years on the bottom. But nothing had grown in the dead waters. The sub lay uncannily clean, like a bone picked bare by some gigantic inhabitant of the loch.

Uncle Richard jetted into the scene. He turned off the propulsion unit and came down on the sub's foredeck, which tilted at a crazy angle. He stood there awhile, peering into a yawning crack just in front of the conning tower. Then he turned, gave an ironic wave to one of the cameras, and sank out of sight into the submarine.

Fell leaned back in his chair, making sure his gun still covered Stephen, Annie, and Hamish, as did Oswald's. Fell hauled a pocket watch out of his vest. "You have to forgive me. Anticipation makes the time go so slowly."

"Maybe it does for you," Stephen said. "Time seems to be flying for me." He checked his watch, glad that at least the raven had been left on its perch in the other room. What time would it be in New York right now? Stephen shook that thought out of his head. No time for daydreams. No time left at all.

"Well, don't stand around there looking uncomfortable,'' Fell said. His cane tapped the cement. "Sit down.''

"I'm fine,'' Annie said.

Fell's hand tightened on his gun. "Sit!''

Annie sat. So did Stephen and Hamish.

"I suppose you're eaten up with curiosity. What did I send Duffy after? What is this mysterious submarine in the loch?'' Fell gave them a laugh, the laugh of a person who's going to tell a story whether anyone wants to hear it or not.

"I'll explain it all to you,'' Fell said. "It will help pass the time.''

"Yeah, we'll just be fascinated,'' Stephen said. Fell gave him an icy look, and Stephen said nothing more.

"It goes back to 1945—the end of the war.'' Fell smiled reminiscently. "I was just a young lieutenant then, with the Occupation forces in Germany.''

"No death merchant?'' Stephen said in spite of himself.

Fell's eyes snapped back into focus. "No smart-mouth from you, boy. It's impudent.'' He smiled again. "As a matter of fact, you could say I was beginning my career. Mountains of captured German weaponry were just waiting for a clever man to do something with them. Officially my job was to go through captured German records. I was a weapons specialist. Do you remember Hitler's 'vengeance weapons'? ''

Annie nodded. "They appeared toward the end of

the war," she said, "when things were going badly for the Germans. There was the V-1, the buzz-bombs, and the V-2, some sort of rockets, weren't they?"

"Very good," Fell said. "Well, I discovered the records for the V-3."

"There never was any V-3," Stephen said. "I've read all about World War II."

"Oh, there was a V-3. It never got used. In the files it was referred to as *Todesstaub*—death dust. Apparently it was a fine powder that killed everything it touched."

Stephen began to see a glimmer of sense in what was going on.

"Those files made very interesting reading, I tell you. I searched all over for the death dust, but couldn't find it. But"—Fell leaned forward—"I did find some more files—tests of the stuff. It was quite deadly, but there was a problem. The stuff was chemically unstable. If the Germans put it in artillery shells, firing the gun destroyed the dust—made it explode, too, rendering it harmless.

"The Germans thought about releasing it into the air from a plane, but it was the same problem as the gas attacks they tried in the first war. The winds usually blow from France into Germany. They didn't want to try that."

"Did your files say what they finally did decide?" Annie asked.

"There was only enough dust for one mission," Fell said. "They loaded all the canisters aboard a

U-boat and sent it off to Britain. The submarine would work its way along the coast until it lay upwind of London, and then release the dust.''

Stephen, Hamish, and Annie sat for a moment, thinking what would have happened.

''Undoubtedly the dust would have wiped out the entire population of London, perhaps even the surrounding counties. But something went wrong. I traced through the files for that submarine. The last record mentioned a stop for supplies in Norway, and that was the end of it.'' Fell smiled. ''For then.''

''I destroyed the files, keeping what was important up here.'' He tapped his temple. ''Did some unauthorized searching through the anti-submarine warfare records when I came back to London. They showed that a submarine had been sighted off the coast of Scotland and apparently sunk—at the same time as the U-boat mission I was interested in. Unfortunately the spotters never pinpointed the location, and they never found any wreckage from the sub.''

Fell shrugged. ''Things stayed at that point for many years. Then, by chance, I happened to read about the Death Loch. A site on the coast of Scotland where everything died—forty years ago.'' He nodded. ''I sent divers into the loch, and they managed to locate the sub.

''But then, the final joke. My men weren't experienced at diving in contaminated water. Several became deathly ill. The rest refused to go into the submarine. It was dangerous enough diving through the diluted death dust in the loch. They figured the stuff was concentrated inside the wreck. Miserable cowards! I'd found the death dust, but couldn't get at it. Even with protective suits, none of my divers would go near it.

"Further complications came then, people poking their noses into the loch. I managed to get rid of the Royal Commission busybodies." Fell smiled at Annie. "All but you, Miss MacKenzie.

"The other meddler was quite interesting—a retired Intelligence man who'd spent as many years as I had searching for the death dust—"

"I'd have had an easier time of it if some blasted villain hadn't kept destroying all the records." Hamish's voice sounded rusty, as if he hadn't used it in some time.

"You were a distinct threat to my project. I had to get you out of the picture," Fell said. "Little did I think that you would have the answer to my problem, until I learned about a friend of yours."

Fell nodded. "Richard Duffy. He'd thwarted me often enough in his adventuring days. He had the talents I needed. I had a friend of his in my power. How delicious to force him into recovering a super-weapon for me! And if he didn't succeed"—Fell smiled—"there would be other ways. The death dust will still be there."

"He's really mad!" Annie whispered, so softly only Stephen could hear her.

Fell dug into his vest again for his watch. "My,

my, I have certainly rambled on!'' He looked at his watch, then closed it with a snap. "I'm afraid I'll have to end this little chat. Your uncle is apparently unable to return.'' His colorless eyes gleamed as he raised his gun. "Your time is up. Just as well, I suppose. You've heard too many secrets.''

15

DEATH DUST!

SUNDAY: 2:54 A.M., *Scotland*

Stephen's mouth went dry as he looked down the barrels of the two guns. Behind Fell and Oswald the television monitors continued to glow. A sudden movement on one of the screens caught Stephen's eye. Uncle Richard was swimming out of the crack in the sunken sub.

"Look behind you—my uncle . . ." Stephen said, pointing at the monitor.

"That is the oldest trick in the book, sonny," Fell said, taking aim. "And I'm not going to fall for it."

"Boy's right." Hamish Claymore's creaky voice rasped out. "Duffy is on those screens."

"Shoot if they try anything funny, Oswald." Fell turned to the screen just in time to see Uncle Richard jetting away. He put his gun down and began fiddling with the camera controls. "Blasted cameras won't give me a clear shot of him." he said. Then he turned around again. "Did you see him? Was he carrying anything?"

"Can't say," Claymore nodded at the gun on him. "I was distracted."

Moments later they heard splashing sounds outside the cave. Fell picked up his gun and hurried to the jagged opening. A shadowy figure showed up against the green glow of the underwater lighting. The propulsion jet swung up from the water and clattered onto the cement.

Uncle Richard slowly pulled himself onto land, dragging a metal canister after him.

Fell greedily eyed the canister. Then he darted an angry glance at Uncle Richard. "You're late!" he barked.

Uncle Richard stood up. His tool kit was missing —so was the underwater flashlight he had carried. One of his air tanks was dented too. "Sorry. Got into a bit of a fix down there." He smiled at Fell. "But what's a minute or two among friends?"

Both Fell and Oswald glowered at him.

"Stop pouting, the two of you. There'll be other executions, I'm sure," Uncle Richard said.

He has something up his sleeve, Stephen thought. If only I could figure out what it is. As far as Stephen could see, the situation was the same. Fell and Oswald still had the guns. The only new thing was the metal canister in Uncle Richard's hand.

"I suppose you're right, Duffy. We can't let our feelings run away with us, eh?" Fell strove to be friendly, but Stephen saw the look flickering in his eyes.

"Well, now." Fell still kept a cheerful note in his voice. "I see you're holding the reason for this whole business." The old man's eyes devoured the metal tube in Uncle Richard's hands.

Uncle Richard tossed the canister in the air and casually caught it in one hand. Everyone in the room jumped back.

"Are you mad!" Fell shrilled. "Do you know what that canister can do?"

"Why, no, I don't," Uncle Richard said. "You never told me."

"It's a German secret weapon from the war," Annie shouted out.

"Death dust! If it gets out, it'll kill everything it touches!" Stephen added.

Uncle Richard whistled, and gave the canister in his hand a respectful look. "So I've got a powerful weapon here . . ."

Fell's pistol pointed at Uncle Richard's head. "If you're thinking of any clever plans, you can just forget them—right now."

Uncle Richard smiled at the gun, then looked Fell in the eye. "I suppose you can shoot me. But then I'm sure to fall . . . and what happens if this oversized tin can bursts open?" He held the canister at chest level, hefting it.

The gun wavered in Fell's hand for a second. Then his eyes sharpened and the gun came up again.

"Almost bluffed me, Duffy, but it won't work. Yes, you have a powerful weapon there, and a problem. To make it work, you would have to die. I'm willing to bet that you don't hate me that much. Besides, you'd have to kill your friend Hamish, Miss MacKenzie, and your nephew to get me. I think you'd find that too high a price."

They looked at each other as seconds ticked away. Finally Uncle Richard shrugged and grinned. "You win, Fell. Now what?"

Fell stood in cold triumph. "Put the canister down on the floor, and step back with the others."

Uncle Richard did as he was commanded.

Fell turned to Oswald. "Pick up the canister."

Oswald froze, staring down on the innocent-looking metal container. "P-p-pick it up, sir?"

"Yes, you fool!" Fell roared in his best drill-field manner. "Put your hands around it and pick it up. Have your wits suddenly deserted you?"

The bodyguard's eyes were glued to the tarnished metal of the canister. "I—I—I . . . how do we know it isn't leaking?"

"Duffy stood there holding it, and he's still alive isn't he, you nit?" Fell's voice slashed at him.

"But he's wearing a protective suit, and—" Oswald's voice took on a whining quality.

"Lower-class trash! Always crying about this and that! It's your sort who lost us the Empire! All right!

Cringe over there with your gun! Keep an eye on the prisoners!'' He stalked over to the canister and bent over. At the last moment a trace of worry appeared in his eyes.

Uh-oh, Stephen thought, what if old Oswald is right?

But with everyone's eyes on him Fell couldn't back down. After a second's hesitation he picked up the canister.

"Have to do things for yourself," he said, sneering at Oswald. "Ah, what a prize this will be. Are there more down there, Duffy? No matter. We can have the contents of this analyzed. . . .'' He was running a caressing hand over the metal of the canister. Suddenly he stopped. "What's this? Lettering engraved on the metal?''

Fell had to squint, leaning close to the surface to read the tarnished writing. "F . . . E . . . U . . ." His eyes blazed with maniacal fury. *"Feuerlöscher!"*

His hands dropped the canister to the floor. Oswald jumped back with a wild cry, but Fell's pistol was rock-steady on Uncle Richard.

"What are you doing?" Oswald squeaked.

"That happens to be the U-boat's fire extinguisher!'' Fell screamed the last words. He took a deep breath, and lowered his voice. "Now I want a real canister.''

Uncle Richard shrugged. "That was the only one in the captain's quarters.''

"Don't lie to me!" Fell shrieked. He stalked across the room and aimed his pistol point-blank at

Uncle Richard's head. "The records said the canisters were to be kept in the captain's cabin until the ship was in striking distance. We saw you go into the sub—the extinguisher shows you were searching. So, *where are the canisters?*" A spray of spittle came from his lips as he yelled.

Uncle Richard just looked at him.

Fell jammed the gun into the side of Uncle Richard's head. "You have three seconds."

Uncle Richard looked at his watch. Fell's eyes bulged in rage. "Don't dream that I'm jesting," he hissed. "One, two . . ." Tightening his hand on the gun, Fell pulled the trigger.

16

UNDER THE GUN

SUNDAY: 3:09 A.M., *Scotland*

A bone-jarring *boom!* came from outside the room. They all gaped as an explosion ripped through the water, hurling up a huge column of spray to soak them.

"But Uncle Richard!" Stephen cried, expecting to see the worst. Instead, he saw his uncle brush past the astonished Fell and tackle Oswald—just as another huge wave swamped the cave floor. Between the sweep of the water and Uncle Richard, Oswald was down before he knew what was happening.

Uncle Richard grabbed Oswald's gun and whipped around to cover Fell. The old man stood trembling, his mouth an *O* of astonishment.

"You need more practice at the shooting range," Uncle Richard said. "That explosion made you flinch.'' His eyes flicked from the powder burn on his shoulder to Fell again. "And I suppose you're wondering what all the commotion outside is about. Well, Jonathan, I have bad news for you. That was a torpedo I rigged aboard the U-boat out in the loch. And carefully arranged around it was the world's supply of death dust.''

Fell's jaw sagged. "B-but you knew nothing about the dust. I told you nothing about its properties.'' His eyes went wild. "How did you know that an explosion would consume it?''

"Hamish told me.''

Fell's mouth worked, but no words came out.

"Take it easy. He told me about ten years ago. You see, Hamish knew about death dust from his Intelligence work during the war. I knew he was looking for a sunken sub with the stuff aboard, since he never made a secret of his project. When I got the cable from him, I wondered if there was any connection to the death dust.

"Then, as we were climbing up your wall, we heard two of your guards talking about a submarine. One mentioned that they couldn't blast around it, or its cargo would be destroyed.'' Uncle Richard smiled at Fell's mad look. "Loose lips sink subs,'' he said.

Fell's face never had much color, but now it went even paler than usual. His stiff British-officer spine seemed to dissolve. A shattered old man suddenly stood before them, head hanging, shoulders stooped. "Forty years of searching . . .'' he said in a broken voice. "To have it destroyed right when it was in my grasp."

Stephen thought Fell was going to burst into tears.

Instead, with a speed that belied his years, he leaped around and grabbed Annie MacKenzie. He spun her in front of him. Then, clutching her neck with one hand, he put his pistol to her temple. "But I can still get revenge!" The colorless eyes now looked totally mad. "Duffy, put down that gun, or your lady friend will be no more."

Staring into Fell's eyes, Uncle Richard knelt and put his gun on the floor.

Fell had a handful of Annie's hair, which he wound around his fingers. "Such lovely red hair," he crooned. "A shame to waste it. Perhaps I'll spare you, my dear, if you beg me to. The others will all have to die of course. But perhaps you can convince me not to give you the treatment you deserve."

Uncle Richard's face twisted as he watched.

"Oh, M-M-Mr. Fell, p-p-please don't kill me, please," Annie said in a high-pitched, hysterical voice. But while her voice was sobbing, her eyes were looking at Uncle Richard. They glanced down to the small specimen pouch at her hip. Moving like a silent spider, her left hand slowly inched its way over to it.

Uncle Richard's eyes flickered for a moment, then went back to Fell's face.

"Upsets you to hear her whine and beg, doesn't it?" Fell smiled nastily. He twisted her hair tighter around his hand. "But you haven't convinced me yet, dear. Perhaps a little more begging would be in order.''

Stephen watched the scene with ice water in his veins. Seeing Fell mistreat Annie was bad enough, but watching the slow progress of her hand was even worse. He had to keep himself from staring at it, from calling Fell's attention to their only hope.

Fell's face didn't quite look human anymore. Little trails of spittle rolled down from the sides of his mouth. And he laughed in a high-pitched cackle.

"Come on, dearie, convince me," he roared, shaking Annie.

"Oooooh, you, you're hurting me, Mr. Fell," she quavered. Her eyes blazed with rage. Her hand was now inside the pouch.

"I'll do worse than that to you, my dear," Fell said. "I'll kill you! I'll kill you all! You all plotted together to ruin my dream! My only regret is you won't feel enough pain when you die!" His eyes shone with unholy light. "You'll be the first to go, Duffy, then the brat. Then old Hamish—that would be a mercy killing, wouldn't it?" He shook Annie again. "And then you, my pretty one."

Her hand was out of the bag, a specimen knife clutched in it. "I don't want to die," she said.

"You monster!" Uncle Richard said in his best melodramatic tone.

Fell turned to laugh at him, and Annie's knife streaked up to plunge into Fell's gun hand. His fingers twitched, and the gun fell.

Stephen darted forward and grabbed it. Uncle Richard scooped up his pistol.

Annie had already twisted free. She turned around on Fell, the knife still in her hand.

Uncle Richard touched her shoulder. "No. Leave it to the police."

The blaze went out of Annie's eyes as she got a good look at the old man, stooped over now, mumbling.

"So much evil," she said. "It burnt itself out."

Suddenly Uncle Richard jerked around. "The townspeople! We've got to get up to the towers! Quick!"

As he dashed through the tunnels, thoughts raced through Stephen's mind. How long was it since the explosion? he wondered. What's going on up there?

Uncle Richard hustled Fell along until they reached the door to the control room. As the door swung open, Stephen saw a crafty glitter in Fell's eyes. He pushed past Uncle Richard, and leaped to the raven perched in the room. Snapping loose the chain, he whirled and pointed. "Attack, Fafnir. Kill!"

17

WHOSE HEART IS IN THE HIGHLANDS?

SUNDAY: 3:25 A.M., *Scotland*

Bunched up in the doorway, there was no way Stephen or the others could avoid the bird. Flying straight at them, it seemed to be all beak and claws.

Uncle Richard pushed his way to the front, raising up his white-bandaged hands. They weren't the huge mittens that had foiled the bird the last time, but the raven remembered. With a wild flutter of wings, it stopped its rush at the door, looking for a better way to attack. "A very intelligent bird," Stephen muttered.

Watching the raven's retreat, Fell misunderstood the hesitation. "At them!" he shouted, slashing at the bird with his cane. "I said attack!"

The raven dodged the cane and launched its attack, but not at Stephen and the others. It attacked the nearer enemy, the one who swung the stick at it. Fell gave a high, shrill scream as claws raked his face, his hands frantically plucking at the bird as it darted around him. The raven seemed to back-pedal in the air with a wild rush of wings. Fell's cane sliced through the air, caught the bird, and smashed it into one of the monitor screens.

The set exploded, disintegrating the screen, the raven, and the end of Fell's cane. Fell stood blinking in the room. Tears ran down beside the scratches on his face. "He turned against me. . . ."

Uncle Richard came up and grabbed Fell's arm. There was no fight left in him at all. Stephen watched his uncle steer Fell out to the stairway. "Come on," he said, "let's move it!"

They met a few guards on their way to the towers, but with Fell in their power, they had no problems. Arriving at the east tower, Stephen heard the commander there arguing with the commander of the other tower. "The chief said we were supposed to hold them—do nothing until we got his orders," East Tower said.

"He hasn't been on the radio to give orders," West Tower answered. "And you still don't have an explanation for that explosion. I say we wipe out these villagers, and get some patrols down to the loch."

Uncle Richard and company burst into the command post. Fell was in the middle of the group, with two pistols shoved into his sides. "Here's the chief," Uncle Richard said. "And if you don't want to send him to his just reward, you'll put up those machine guns and open the castle gates.''

The gates opened, and the villagers poured into the castle. Harry MacGeachin led the group that came to take over the towers. "That was the longest half hour of my life," Harry declared. "Now I know how a fish in a net feels."

Uncle Richard turned over the guards' weapons. "Sorry for the delay, Harry. We got detained."

When all the men in the castle were under guard, Uncle Richard explained what had happened.

". . . So after I found the canisters in the Captain's quarters, I brought them all to the forward torpedo room. It wasn't too hard to disassemble one of the torpedos. And with the battery from my flashlight, I had the makings of a bomb. If my tanks hadn't gotten caught on some debris, I'd have been back with time to spare."

"Instead, you grabbed up a fire extinguisher and rushed back to us," Annie said.

"And just in time too," Stephen put in.

Uncle Richard shrugged. "It was the only thing handy that looked like a canister. I was a little worried, figuring that Fell might recognize it right away. But he was looking for a canister, and that's what he thought it was, thank goodness."

"What luck," Stephen said.

"You mean, what a clever plan," Uncle Richard said.

Stephen grinned. "If you say so."

"Now, what do we do with all these prisoners?" Harry wanted to know.

"I can show you some nice, secure rooms to lock them up in." Hamish Claymore's voice came from behind them. "I've just been on the radio—talking to some friends in Intelligence. They'll be here soon to clean up all of this."

"And all those fellas who are out searching?" one of the villagers asked.

'We'll disarm them as they come back to the castle," Hamish said. "They're really nothing by themselves. We've gotten the head here, that's the important thing."

"That's the way Fell put it. Cut off the head, and you're in the clear," Stephen said.

Annie MacKenzie came over and linked her arm through Uncle Richard's. "My, and it's a mighty man you are, Richard Duffy, freein' the people from the dread tyrant Fell." She grinned.

Uncle Richard grinned back. "Och, I wouldn't have been doin' any such thing without the strong left hand of Annie MacKenzie."

"But it was your Great White Hands that defeated the Raven Maniac," Stephen put in.

They all laughed, but Stephen noticed the way Annie and Uncle Richard looked into each other's eyes.

"A lot has happened since I bumped into you on the lochside," Uncle Richard said quietly.

"It all moved so quickly," Annie said. "I still hardly know you." She looked down. "But I want to get to know you."

"I'd like that, but there's no way I can stay here right now. . . ."

Suddenly, from down the loch, came the lonely sound of a train whistle. Uncle Richard's head snapped up. "What's that?"

"It's the train to Inverness," Annie said.

"That can't be!" Uncle Richard looked at his watch. "Where could the time have gone?"

"I guess you'll have to stay for a while. There's no train until ten in the morning." Annie smiled at him. But the smile faded when she saw the look on Uncle Richard's and Stephen's faces.

"We got . . . a little caught up in things, didn't we?" Stephen said. "Best watches in the world aren't any help if you don't pay attention to them." He wet his lips. "The folks are due back tomorrow—this afternoon. And we've got a dozen-hour trip before we get there. I guess we're really stuck, unless you have a plan."

Uncle Richard shook his head. "This time I don't even have a ghost of one." He winced. "Oh, is your mother going to be mad."

A huge racket in the sky drowned out whatever he was going to say. Stephen stared up. The moon had set, but now bright lights moved against the backdrop of the stars. "What the—" he said. "A helicopter!"

People scattered around the castle courtyard as the

copter came in for a landing. Uncle Richard came up as the pilot stuck his head out of the bubble. "Hey, mate, don't you know you're supposed to have a bloke on the radio when you're expecting a helicopter?"

Uncle Richard stared at him.

"Look, this is Raven Castle, ain't it? You got a Mr. Fell around this pile somewhere?" The pilot pulled a sheet of paper from his pocket. "I'm supposed to bring a bunch of sealed canisters down to Inverness for analysis—that's what it says here."

Uncle Richard suddenly found his voice. "Sorry, there's been a change of plans. No canisters. You'll be carrying two passengers to Inverness instead." He turned around. "Steve, over here—quick."

Stephen ran to the helicopter. From behind him he heard Annie running too. "You're leaving then?" she blurted out, then bit her lip.

"Annie, I don't want to. I *have* to. I wish . . . I want . . . oh, heck!" He threw his arms around her and kissed her. Annie turned as red as her hair while the townspeople applauded.

"I'll be back to Killy Bay, I promise," Uncle Richard said.

"Well, I won't be here," Annie said.

Uncle Richard's face fell.

"The secret of the Death Loch is solved. They'll need chemists to figure out how to fix it." She grinned. "But if you're ever in Edinburgh"—she whipped a card out of her wallet and stuck it in Uncle Richard's pocket—you might give me a call." Then she flung her arms around Uncle Richard and kissed him back. "I hope you do."

"Count on it!" he said.

Already strapped in his seat, Stephen looked out from the bubble of the helicopter. "Hey, Uncle Richard!" he called.

Uncle Richard gave Annie a hug and ran for the helicopter. Moments later they took off, as the villagers cheered and waved.

The helicopter headed straight up, then made a circle around the castle. As it did, its landing lights caught two figures stealthily climbing down a crevice in the castle's walls. One of them was a big, stocky man—the other, thin and fox-faced. They gaped up at the helicopter.

"Uncle Richard, look!" Stephen yelled over the clatter of the rotor blades. "It's Dougal and Davey trying to get away! Shouldn't we stop them?"

Uncle Richard sat there, grinning like a fool. "I feel too good to chase them. Let them get away and wreck some other gang!"

18

"AND I'LL BE HAME AFORE YE"

SUNDAY: 12:02 A.M., *New York*

The trip back to New York came to Stephen only in flashes. Most of the time he kept dozing off. He did remember Uncle Richard having a loud fight over the radio with one of his contacts about changing his flight plans. And on the plane ride from Inverness to London, the crew kept giving them dirty looks. They had been held up waiting for Stephen and Uncle Richard to arrive.

Stephen also remembered the funny looks he and his uncle had gotten when they boarded the Concorde at Heathrow Airport—two grubby-looking figures walking onto the ultra-expensive aircraft. Uncle Richard hadn't cared, and Stephen had been too tired.

When they got to Kennedy in New York, they both looked a lot more respectable. Uncle Richard

134

had shaved and washed up during the flight, and Stephen even combed his hair. After sleeping for almost the whole flight, he felt bright and chipper as their cab fought the traffic into the city. Uncle Richard looked like he hadn't slept a wink.

"I'm worried. I wish we had a better idea about when your folks were arriving . . . something better than 'sometime Sunday afternoon.' "

Stephen looked at his watch. "It's Sunday afternoon already."

"I'm only too aware of that," Uncle Richard said. He went back to fretting silently. His bandages looked pretty ratty now. By the time they reached the Fifty-ninth Street bridge, he'd managed to pick them completely apart.

"Those scratches don't look so bad," Stephen said.

"I'll have to get this wrist looked at though. I hope that's all." Uncle Richard looked over at Stephen's concerned face. "If your mother finds out what we were up to, the doctor might wind up with a lot more business. When she gets angry . . . well, I once saw her chase a guy for half a mile with a baseball bat."

"Why?"

Uncle Richard looked sheepish. "He was teasing me."

They sat in gloomy silence for a moment. "This whole thing is my fault, dragging you off to Scotland on another nutty adventure."

"I wouldn't have gone if I didn't want to," Stephen said. "Besides, look what Harry MacGeachin gave me." He held up a multicolored piece of fluff.

Uncle Richard peered at it. "Okay, I give up. What is it?"

"It's a fishing fly. Harry makes them. Isn't it neat? It will go with that great videocassette Jack Hartford gave me as a souvenir of our Sahara adventure."

Uncle Richard gave a half-hearted grin. "I think I detect the beginning of a collection here."

Traffic on the bridge was terrible. "Of all the days to work on the roads, why do they have to pick Sunday?" Uncle Richard fumed.

"That's the day there's the least traffic, mac," the cab driver said.

"The least traffic—until it gets all jammed up." Uncle Richard sent a black look out the window. Then he suddenly slumped in his seat.

"Steve," he hissed. "Take a quick look out the window, then get down!"

Stephen glanced out the rear window. Another cab was crawling along with them. Two people sat in the back—Mom and Dad. He ducked down, his eyes big. "What are we going to do?"

"Take it easy; they haven't seen us yet."

"Yeah, but they will, and think of all the questions Mom will ask when she sees us coming out of a cab," Stephen groaned.

"Let's not give up yet," Uncle Richard said. "I have a plan. Driver?" he called.

"What is it, mac?" The driver looked around for Uncle Richard. "Whattaya doin' down there?"

"How would you like to make an extra ten out of this job?"

"Always happy. How?"

"Don't take us up First Avenue to Sixty-first Street. Swing round to Third, and take us up that way—as fast as you can."

"But that's the long way around . . ." The driver shrugged. "You're the boss."

They pulled away from Mom and Dad's cab. Stephen turned to Uncle Richard. "But if we take the long way around, they'll be home before us."

"Don't bet on it," Uncle Richard said. "That end of Sixty-first Street is clogged with construction."

They were soon heading up Third, but got caught at a light about a block and a half from home. Uncle Richard shoved a pile of bills over the seat. "We'll get out here." He opened the door.

The cab driver looked at the money. "Hey . . ."

"Keep the change," Uncle Richard said, already hustling down the street.

Stephen had to stretch his legs to catch up with his uncle. They charged down the street, dodging people. In the distance was home—Number 224 ½. "Everything looks okay. No cab . . . unless they're inside already."

They puffed up the front steps. Stephen fumbled for

his house key in his pocket and put it into the lock. It wouldn't turn. He froze for a second. "I used it to scrape around the bar in Fell's castle. Now it won't work!" He tried to remove it from the lock. The key wouldn't move at all. "Jammed!"

Uncle Richard tore the key out and used his own. The door swung open and they were inside. They heard a car pull up. One glance out the window to make sure it was a taxi, and then they were dashing up the stairs as the doorbell rang.

Stephen went to answer it. "Here we are," Mom said, hugging him. Uncle Richard came down the stairs.

"Hello, Marion," he said.

Mom looked them over. "What were you doing, out playing in the park? Your clothes are all grubby." Her face got stern. "I hope you weren't playing too rough."

Dad came walking up, puffing under the weight of the suitcases. "What a wasted weekend," he complained. "I met with these guys at Fell Industries, and they couldn't understand a thing I was talking about." He ran a hand through his thinning hair. "You'd think the big boss had asked them just to take up my time."

"We did get to see San Francisco," Mom said.

"That was great, but I had hoped to do some business with them," Dad said.

"Probably just as well. It didn't register when you mentioned the company, but now I remember hearing they were in for some legal trouble soon," said Uncle Richard.

"Oh, really?" Dad said. "Probably just as well then." He looked from the suitcases to the stairway. "Think you could give me a hand with these, Richard? They always seem heavier coming home than they do going away."

"I—uh . . ." Uncle Richard looked down at his hands. That's when Mom got her first view of the scratches.

"Richard Duffy, what have you done to yourself?" she said, grabbing his right hand for a better look.

Uncle Richard turned bright pink and stuttered like a kid. "I—I skinned my palms . . . fell down. Jogging. It's really nothing."

"Probably trying to impress your nephew." She snorted. "Honestly, you can be worse than a child sometimes." Still holding his hand, she marched into the house. "Well, come in and let's get those hands cleaned up. Stephen, you help your father with the bags."

Uncle Richard followed meekly along behind her to the bathroom—and the medicine cabinet—and no doubt, a stern lecture.

Stephen grinned at the retreating back of his uncle, then straightened his face as he turned to Dad. "Well, let's get those suitcases," he said.

As they started up the steps, his father looked at him. "I was thinking about you in San Francisco," Dad said. "Wondering if you were feeling a bit jealous that your mother and I were having all the excitement.''

''Nah. Being with Uncle Richard was enough excitement for me.'' Stephen carefully kept his eyes on the suitcases. Otherwise he was afraid he'd explode with laughter.

Behold a bold new world of adventure

Jam-packed with danger, suspense, and intrigue, RACE AGAINST TIME pits teenage Stephen Lane and his handsome bachelor uncle, Richard, against ruthless enemies in exotic lands. Chased, trapped, and pushed to the edge of death, they *always* survive, due in no small part to their secret weapon—a pair of Kronom KD2 computer watches.

Look for a total of 10 paperbacks in 1984, numbers 1-4 coming in January.